THE LAW OF CHAOS
the Multiverse of Michael Moorcock

by
Jeff Gardiner

HEADPRESS

CONTENTS

Dedicated to Sandy, Emily and Bethany.

AUTHOR'S PREFACE

The Law of Chaos: the Multiverse of Michael Moorcock was previously published in 2002 as *The Age of Chaos* by the British Fantasy Society, to whom I am grateful for their support of this work. The title has reverted to my original and preferred 'Law of Chaos', whose paradoxical tone better reflects the tension of opposites in Moorcock's multiversal balance.

This edition contains a number of revisions, expansions, updated clarifications and new material. Moorcock's novels published since 2002, such as *The Vengeance of Rome* are now added to the discussion — plus a chapter on Oswald Bastable, whose previous omission had lost me many a night's sleep. More has been included on Moorcock's non-fiction, particularly his work as an editor. The appendices include previously unpublished and lengthy letters from Moorcock plus a previously unseen interview. The bibliography has been heavily revised and reorganised as a reader's guide, noting original editions and dates. I also include here a short essay examining Moorcock and Robert Calvert's lyrics for the rock band Hawkwind.

I would like to thank David Mosley, John Davey and David Kerekes for helping me with this book. A mention should also go to artist Malcolm Laverty who has provided me with a number of illustrations used in this revised edition.

My biggest thanks, though, go to Michael Moorcock himself for his generous and lengthy introduction. He continues to be patient, polite and never patronising even when asked the same old questions over and again. Thanks, Mike, for all the dreams, laughter, shocks, challenges, inspiration and entertainment you've provided over the years. The very best of health to you, sir!

Jeff Gardiner, 2014

'The idea of a "quasi-infinite" series of interlocking worlds, each a fraction different from the next, where millions of versions of our realities are played out, fascinated me from the age of seventeen.'

Moorcock's introduction to
Michael Moorcock's Multiverse no. 1 (DC Comics 1997)

INTRODUCTION BY MICHAEL MOORCOCK

How do you judge a book which is about yourself? Naturally, if it is kind, you are flattered. Then you are concerned that it doesn't somehow misrepresent you and that it has its facts right, and then you read it to see if it offers you any fresh ideas on your own stuff. Jeff Gardiner's excellent book has offered me many fresh insights into my own work and it will remain, for me at least, a very useful reference when I have one of those increasingly frequent moments of not knowing what's going on in my own fiction, let alone my life.

I don't have a habit of rereading my own work and so much of Jeff Gardiner's detailed study is pretty fresh to me. I feel, therefore, that I can recommend it as a pretty useful guide to the variety of fiction I've turned out over a fifty-seven-year career as a professional writer. Whether it is of any use to other writers, they will know best, but I think it should help the casual reader to get a better grip on the vast raft of stuff I've produced and also, I hope, give them an idea about what they would like to read and what doesn't interest them.

I must admit I pity any reader coming to my work for the first time and wondering where on earth they should begin. It tends to baffle me, let alone them. And when I am asked to recommend something of my own, I find it very hard to do. Readers who love *Mother London*, for instance, might not care for *The Sundered Worlds* at all and Hawkmoon fans might be bored to the teeth with *King of the City*. My father's personal favourite of mine was *Kane of Old Mars*, which was closest to the Edgar Rice Burroughs romances I first started reading in his copies.

I have an old-fashioned idea about my profession. I believe I should be able to turn my hand to almost any form at the drop of a hat — belles-lettres, criticism, fiction of various kinds, film scripts,

3

TV work, short stories, novels, reminiscence, music and lyrics, whatever you can do. I think that some ideas are best expressed in semi-fiction, some in fiction, some in non-fiction and so on. Genres present their own methods. You use the best tools for the job. Some ideas are more suitable for essays, some for fiction. I also have ideas for novels which suit certain methods or express certain ideas best. I have written spoof detective stories, westerns and fantasy stories. I have written mostly non-modernist literary fiction but on occasions I have used modernist techniques because they are best suited to what I have to say. I have a habit of putting some of my most thoughtful notions into comic books.

Until recently, my best description of 'the multiverse' was in the DC graphic novel, *Michael Moorcock's Multiverse*, which a number of my readers found impossible to understand. There is a way of reading a modern graphic novel which, to some degree, you have to learn, just as children have to learn the sequence of an ordinary sentence. Equally, there is a specialist vocabulary in fantasy and science fiction circles which often baffles the casual reader and indeed can act to alienate them from work they might otherwise enjoy. For this reason, I tend to start every fantasy book I write as if neither I nor my reader had read a fantasy novel before. I believe this helps to keep the book's vitality and interest, as well as being generally more user friendly! This method tends to give me, as far as I can tell, a slightly broader general audience than the average genre writer while making me slightly marginal to the genre audience, who are sometimes suspicious of what they might see as my divided loyalties!

Whatever my qualities as a writer, I am hard to pigeonhole. Critics who see me as 'sampling' different genres don't quite understand that I am not much interested in the genres themselves, just what the genres can offer me. While I've written Kit Carson and Buffalo Bill stories for juvenile weeklies, my adult ventures into their galloping grounds have been satirical or making some specific use of the local mythology. I actually have very little nostalgia for adventure fiction and my own leisure reading tends to be the likes of Elizabeth Bowen, Elizabeth Taylor and Angus Wilson. I can get very enthusiastic about *Death of the Heart* but remembered a short while ago that I never actually finished *Lord of the Rings*. I still don't know how it ends. This means that I have very few adult enthusiasms within the fantasy and SF genres, though I do greatly admire individual writers like M. John Harrison who write their own highly idiosyncratic fiction and who are as hard to pigeonhole as I am.

I know that I'm a bit of an academic's nightmare. Add to my various literary enthusiasms, my musical career and my career as an editor of a fairly wide variety of publications, and it's no surprise to me to hear that some researchers and writers have actually lost their sanity before they could finish their bibliographies of my stuff, let alone begun their theses. Sometimes just finding the more obscure bits and pieces themselves is daunting and I am of no use, being bad at dates and record-keeping in general. For that reason, if no other, I can genuinely celebrate the publication of this book. It lifts some of my own confusion and I'm pretty sure it will lift some of yours. I welcome its publication especially since its author still manages to retain a convincing veneer of sanity and is, by all accounts, recovering well.

Michael Moorcock, 2012

PRELUDE

Fantasy writer Angela Carter called Michael Moorcock 'the master Storyteller of our time' — a well-deserved title for an author who has influenced the literary world for well over fifty years. Carter, herself an avid reader of Moorcock, was keen to celebrate the importance of Moorcock's work. In her enthusiastic review of *Mother London* in the *Guardian*, she concludes that: 'Posterity will certainly give him that due place in the English literature of the late twentieth century which his more anaemic contemporaries grudge; indeed, he is so prolific it will probably look as though he has written most of it anyway'. Michael Moorcock is one of Britain's greatest writers and he is possibly the most consistently experimental author in the world of fantasy literature. Not only did he practically invent modern British fantasy and reshape science fiction as an editor, but he is also an exponent of mainstream literature. While he, ironically, rejects the notion of being a genre writer, he is probably most famous for his fantasy hero Elric the albino, and for the science fiction icon of 1960s psychedelia, Jerry Cornelius.

In *The Encyclopaedia of Fantasy*, John Clute calls Moorcock, 'the most important UK fantasy author of the 1960s and 1970s'. This is misleading, as he continues to write prolifically into the twenty-first century and it could be argued that his later novels are amongst his best work. Clute does, however, suggest that Moorcock is 'altogether the most significant UK author of sword and sorcery' and it is probably for his interlinking *Eternal Champion* novels that he will be most widely remembered. The extent of Moorcock's popularity is demonstrated by his worldwide following, led by an active international appreciation society, The Nomads of the Time Streams, and by the fact that his work is translated into many languages. Type his name into any search engine on the internet and you will encounter innumerable web sites that pay homage to him. What is most impressive about Michael Moorcock is that he has continued to produce novels, stories and non-fiction to such a high standard.

Michael Moorcock has won two World Fantasy Awards, including one in 2000 for Lifetime Achievement; a Nebula award; the Guardian Fiction Prize; a John W. Campbell Memorial Award and even a nomination for the Whitbread Prize. He also has a collection of six British Fantasy Awards: four August Derleth Awards, one for the short story category and, of course, the 1992 Special Award for his Lifetime Achievement. In 2002 he was inducted into the Science Fiction and Fantasy Hall of Fame. Moorcock has about 100 books to his name, some of which are republished and retitled editions of earlier works, and this can prove bewildering to the uninitiated. My own attempt to bring a semblance of order to this chaos can be found in my Moorcock bibliography at the back of this book.

While his books are still categorised under fantasy or SF, this doesn't fully represent his whole oeuvre, which is perhaps better labelled as slipstream or fantastic realism. Moorcock has written about fantasy forms in literature in his book, *Wizardry and Wild Romance,* one of the best books about fantasy by a fantasist, and he both acknowledges and proves through his own writing that fantasy is an important and often under-valued art form. Fantasy creates a tension between what is real and unreal, and this echoes Moorcock's balance between law and chaos. While Moorcock acknowledges the part that fantasy has played in his own success he does admit: 'I have difficulty defining "Fantasy" as a readily definable genre — or frequently even as an element. I don't believe that any technique or method is more or less useful than another — everything depends upon individual human talent in the end.'

His dislike for generic terms is expressed in the following way: 'I don't believe there is such a thing as fantasy or science fiction or detective fiction and so on. I think there are certain writers who in their field shine and in every one of those fields you'll get some good writers emerging. Sometimes the field itself can limit the writer's work and then frequently the writer does something about it.' [1]

Moorcock is a protean writer, whose work transcends literary and generic boundaries; like Charles Dickens, his novels are, paradoxically, both popular and literary. His writing covers fields as far ranging as romance, heroic fantasy, science fiction, fabulation, surrealism, popular fiction, satire, allegory, fantastic realism, postmodernism, magic realism, non-fiction, rock'n'roll, comics and even cinema. His novels defy categorisation because they are greater than the limitations of the critic's vocabulary. As a 'literary' writer Moorcock shows artistic ability in his myth-making and story-telling; his creation of intriguing characters; the subtle irony and ornate vocabulary; an exploitation of metaphor and allegory; and his presentation of imaginary landscapes and emotional relationships. However, his greatest desire is to be a popular author.

He first came to prominence in 1964 as the editor of *New Worlds* magazine with his radical editorial approach that alienated many science fiction fans, but also won him great respect as a writer of vision whose vocabulary and ideas were second to none. His own early stories best exemplify his desire to experiment with structures, themes and language. It was in these early stories that he began to develop the symbolism and subjects that continue to dominate his later writings.

Michael Moorcock is incredibly prolific and what causes the most confusion is the interlinking nature of all his novels. Most of his books fit into a particular mythos or are related to a series of novels, although which one or how is not always immediately obvious. Beginning with a brief autobiographical sketch, this book examines Moorcock's early career as an editor for the avant-garde literary magazine *New Worlds*, and then evaluates his early fantasy and the famous world of Jerry Cornelius that arose from the magazine. Then each chapter discusses a major work or series and attempts to do so in chronological order; that is, by the date of the first book in each series. Any confusion might be caused by the fact that Moorcock does not write his books in any seemingly logical order, and so many of his novels and short stories are repackaged and reprinted.

In this book you will find biographical detail, because to appreciate Moorcock's work means understanding the writer. Moorcock's influence on speculative fiction is evaluated and the *Eternal Champion* — Elric, Corum, Hawkmoon, Ereköse and von Bek — is assessed. Also examined are Jerry Cornelius, the spoof messiah of swinging London; the alternate worlds of Oswald Bastable; the comic fantasy of *The Dancers at the End of Time; Gloriana*; the crazed memoirs of Colonel Pyat; the fantastic realism of *Mother London* and its sequel, *King of the City*; and finally some of Moorcock's later works.

The purpose of this book is to celebrate the achievements of one of literature's leading figures. Fans should find the work a useful tool to explore the multiverse even further and those who are new to Moorcock's work might catch a glimpse of the inspiration behind his mercurial mind. Moorcock successfully creates memorable characters and mystical landscapes using irrepressible wit and exotic language, reminding us all just how fantasy continues to be one of literature's sharpest tools, as well as the key to developing the imagination.

1: THE MASTER STORYTELLER
'MUCH OF MY OWN STUFF SEEMS AT LEAST AS RELEVANT NOW AS IT EVER WAS.' [2]

Born in Mitcham, South London in 1939, Michael Moorcock was a child of the war. He remembers exploring bombed buildings, playing in air-raid shelters and watching dog-fights in the sky. These vivid memories deeply influenced his imagination and the ruined landscapes would be used later in his descriptions of war-torn cities in his heroic fantasies, as well as in *Mother London*. Moorcock admits that his 'futuristic landscapes are symbolic portrayals of the London blitz'. [3]

The Second World War had a huge impact on his life and on much of his writing. His childhood became a series of crazy experiences, seeming normal to a London boy in the forties who considered the destruction and chaos around him 'a wonderland'. He even recalls witnessing the Blitz: 'Bombs fell, landscapes changed, and occasionally I was even allowed to watch from a darkened room as the searchlights roamed across clouds and silvery barrage balloons, seeking targets.' War-torn London became a playground to explore, with young Michael searching for 'shrapnel... perhaps even pistols we could scavenge.' [4]

Some of his recollections are more specific — and from an excited boy's perspective: 'my heart would leap with pleasure at the sound of the aircraft siren, warning us of an attack ...we were forced to descend into the underground... It would mean I could sleep on a platform'. Then one incident convinced him that war could have its uses: 'Over the weekend a V2 dropped out of a pale and silent sky and eliminated the school. I was free.' In fact, war brought colour, danger and excitement to his childhood and Moorcock confesses that 'my life felt dull after the war's end. I had become used to metamorphosis, of almost constantly changing landscapes, of being able to see for miles. I had become used to the adrenaline rush of the bombing raids and the exploration of tottering ruins, of squeezing up through chimneys, of clambering walls whose only handholds were pits in the brick.'

He was disappointed when the war ended, which meant the end of great adventure, excitement and stories of glory and heroism. (Moorcock's guardian, Ernst Jellinek, risked his own life helping Jews escape from the Nazis in Germany and Austria.) No surprise, his unusual childhood proved to be an enormous influence on him. The marriage of his Jewish mother to his Protestant father wasn't altogether successful: 'My father disappeared when I was five, and his family found me an embarrassment'. However, Moorcock remembers the incident philosophically: 'I felt no pain at his departure, probably because he lacked the nerve to tell me he was leaving.' Looking back now Moorcock acknowledges, 'I mostly remember my father in terms of the Christmas presents he gave me — his own collection of cigarette cards, his own toy soldiers... the tricycle...' Thus he admits that he 'grew up in what was essentially a matriarchy', closely bonding with his mother — 'Dark eyed, loving beauty. My constant'.

The young Michael was sent away to school. A couple of formative years were spent at the Michael Hall Steiner Waldorf School in Forest Row, Sussex. Steiner schools emphasise the spiritual, physiological and artistic aspects of education and prefer to think of learning as a mystical journey for each pupil, who is very much an individual. Moorcock states that 'my school did actually shape my life.' The 'cosmic Christianity' taught there not only encouraged his wild imagination but also inspired many of his ideas for the 'multiverse', which he was later to develop through his writing. The young Michael was expelled for his attempted escapes and for storytelling, which were a result of his youthful exuberance and overactive imagination. He was reading classics and popular literature from an early age and would entertain his dormitory at night with fantastic tales. He professes having an early love for Charles Dickens, Edith Nesbitt, ER Burroughs and H Rider Haggard, amongst others. Later influences included Mervyn Peake, George Meredith and Fritz Leiber. Moorcock claims to have read George Bernard Shaw at the age of five.

Moorcock admits to being a precocious child, reading books beyond his years, although his education became complicated and a little difficult. Rather than find success at school, 'Circumstances made me something of an autodidact, unable to settle at any school for very long, expelled from a couple.' Heuristic learning is a method championed by Rudolf Steiner who wrote: 'I am only free when I produce these (moral mental) pictures, not when all I can do is carry out the motives someone else has implanted in me.' This belief still echoes in Moorcock's anarchistic, anti-authoritarian leanings.

Like most young people, Moorcock found himself confused and searching for an identity. 'For half my youth I yearned to be riding some strange, complaining reptilian steed across the dead sea bottoms of Mars while for the other half I longed to be wearing a trench coat, a snap-brim fedora and walking the rain-sodden streets of the big city.' This explains a great deal about the man who on the one hand is a writer of visionary literature while on the other is steeped in popular culture. Fantasy and science fiction appealed to his imagination, but Moorcock was always just as interested in history, world politics, popular music, modern culture and being a fashionable dandy — a man of his time.

While at school he was already typing his own fanzines, the first being *Outlaw's Own* in 1949, written at the age of nine, followed by several others including *Book Collector's News* and eighteen issues of *Burroughsania* on Edgar Rice Burroughs and related authors. Before he left school aged fifteen he was already a serious book collector with useful contacts in publishing and bookselling, and had written his first novel, *The Hungry Dreamers* — a self-indulgent piece of adolescent juvenilia about life in Soho, which was never sent to a publisher but got left for years, during which it was stored in a Ladbroke Grove basement where it was eaten by rats. He left school with typing skills as his only useful qualification.

His first jobs were all in London and included being a messenger for a shipping company and then an office boy for a firm of management consultants, a job that allowed him to continue printing fanzines using the company equipment. At sixteen he was asked to write a heroic fantasy story for a comic magazine, and his Sojan stories, which owe something to Edgar Rice Burroughs and Robert Howard's Conan, were accepted. At the age of seventeen he became the full-time editor of *Tarzan Adventures* on a wage of £6 a week, and was writing comic strips for Kit Carson, Billy the Kid, and other heroes of *Lion* and *Tiger* annuals.

Finding success through jobs, music and writing so young made him consider his image — as everyone did in London in the fifties, and with this in mind, Moorcock 'affected what I hoped was a pale and interesting look. I was regarded as a bit of an enfant terrible'. London became his stomping ground and he fully immersed himself in the pub and café culture where 'A Eurasian whore from Hong Kong might befriend me or an Australian stevedore offer to introduce me to the pleasures of opium.' His upbringing in trendy West London directly inspired the novels of Jerry Cornelius 'whose name was pinched from a greengrocer's sign in Notting Hill'.

By the time he was twenty, Moorcock had joined the Sexton Blake Library as editor. At least one book under this imprint, *Caribbean Crisis*, was written fully by him, but attributed to the house pseudonym, Desmond Reid. The political emphasis, however, was completely reversed. This much sought-after novella (available to read on the internet) is a typical Sexton Blake mystery in which the indomitable hero prevents a communist revolution on a Caribbean island.

Moorcock's first story published under his own name was a collaboration with author Barrington Bayley called 'Peace on Earth', printed in *New Worlds Science Fiction* magazine in 1959. The next breakthrough occurred when the editor of *New Worlds Science Fiction*, Ted Carnell, commissioned from Moorcock a fantasy series for a sister magazine, *Science Fantasy*. This was to be the series that introduced Elric the albino, arguably Moorcock's most popular and enduring character. Carnell also commissioned *Aspects of Fantasy*, a series of informative polemics that would later form the basis of *Wizardry and Wild Romance*. Moorcock states, 'My fantasy stories were to a degree an attempt to demonstrate points I was making in the articles.' For example, a story called 'Sundered Worlds', published in *Science Fiction Adventures* in 1962, first introduced the concept of the multiverse as a series of alternate worlds.

Still in his early twenties Moorcock left his employers to become a full-time writer and journalist, then for a while worked in politics as a staff editor and writer for the Liberal Party. He also travelled widely, drank extensively, and even claims to have had visions when he was ill, seeing images of Christ or buildings shimmering, which he insists were not aided by hallucinogens. Moorcock's lifestyle could be called bohemian and he had long admired the liberal aestheticism of John Ruskin and the pale Epicureanism of the fin-de-siècle. Moorcock's lifestyle at this time is best described as one of sensuality and excess.

He was an obsessive writer; sometimes writing 100 pages a day if necessary, although he found scripting comic strips more financially rewarding than novel writing. He realised that he could earn as much as £50 in one day, but unfortunately he also had the inclination and capacity to drink it all the next. He also experimented with drugs, mostly reefers and acid, but always insisted that drugs should be used responsibly and that they were useless as aids to writing.

Just like his fiction, Michael Moorcock's non-fiction is unwieldy and almost impossible to categorise. Since the 1950s he's covered a number of subjects, particularly literature, politics and feminism, for his own magazines as well as for the *Guardian*, *Daily Telegraph*, *New Statesman, Spectator, LA Times* and *Punch*, among others.

London Peculiar and Other Nonfiction (2012) is an excellent collection of many of Michael Moorcock's essays, reviews, introductions, diaries, obituaries and polemical journalism. He began his writing career as a journalist and claims the skills he developed in this discipline gave him the perfect basis for his fictional structuring and his ability, when younger, to write epic fantasy at an alarming rate.

In April 1963, Moorcock was asked to contribute a guest editorial to *New Worlds* , and at the age of twenty-three was invited to succeed Carnell as full-time editor. He continued until 1974 (issues 142-207) and then later came back intermittently. An important post, editorship at *New Worlds* allowed him to be critical of the existing literary establishment and to experiment with forms and styles in his own writing. This is explored in greater detail in the next chapter.

During this fertile period two notable experimental Moorcock novels came to prominence: *The Final Programme* (1968), the first Jerry Cornelius novel, which subsequently became a film (Goodtime Films, directed by Robert Fuest in 1973) and *Behold The Man* (1969), which had won the Nebula Award as a novella in 1966. Meanwhile he was also developing his *Eternal Champion* stories for the magazine *Science Fantasy*, of which the characters Erekosë and Elric were particularly popular. Most of these stories were adapted into novels, giving Moorcock some financial security and finding a particularly profitable market in America. *New Worlds* was successful under his editorship and achieved its aims of discovering new talent and establishing innovative writing, but its publication became an exhausting task for Moorcock, who was paying for it from his own pocket and finding himself both emotionally and physically drained. Its distributor went bankrupt and even a small Arts Council grant was not enough to run an ambitious magazine. Moorcock published Brian Aldiss' novel *Report On Probability A* in 1967, a novel considered too risky for publication by Faber and Faber, and the magazine subsequently changed format.

New Worlds nurtured what is now known as the new wave of speculative fiction; a movement of sorts, which created such high feeling that it sometimes sparked fighting in the staff offices. Moorcock practically ran things single-handedly for ten years before he handed over the editorship, although he retained ownership of the title. Since the demise of the magazine in 1979, *New Worlds* has continued to exist as an occasional anthology of new short stories or special issues, such as the Fiftieth Anniversary Edition.

Another source of income for Moorcock came from his music, and in the fifties and sixties there was a strong link between science fiction and rock'n'roll. Moorcock played guitar and banjo semi-professionally with a skiffle band, the Greenhorns. He also performed in various other groups, enough to get a taste of the music scene as it began erupting in the early sixties with its bohemian lifestyle around Soho. Embracing the burgeoning pop and folk music subcultures, he earned extra cash 'by playing guitar for a while in a whores' hotel.' He travelled and played abroad, particularly in Sweden and Paris, where he ended up starved and penniless. Moorcock saw himself as a good banjo player. Then the 1970s saw Moorcock involved with London's Ladbroke Grove psychedelic scene, where such stars as David Bowie, Marc Bolan, the Clash and Jimi Hendrix hung out: 'In the early 1970s, Ladbroke Grove was and still is crammed with rock'n'roll people and it was almost impossible not to know at least half a dozen musicians who were either already famous or would soon become famous.' He joined the band Hawkwind and rock music seemed to provide a fresh impetus for his writing.

Hawkwind are still seen by many as the champions of hippy space rock and, having met Robert Calvert their lead singer through the underground magazine, *Frendz*, Moorcock performed with them at a number of concerts, frequently standing in for the unstable Calvert. He recalls, 'I was helping... put on concerts under the motorway in Portobello Road — my first performance with Hawkwind was at one of these gigs, and at that first performance I did Sonic Attack.' His contribution can be heard on several Hawkwind albums, including *Warrior on the Edge of Time* (1975) and *Live Chronicles* (1994), performing his poetry, and writing lyrics for others, such as *Choose Your Masques* (1980). The 1985 album, *The Chronicle of the Black Sword*, was based wholly on the Elric mythos. Hawkwind have a huge cult following and the band still play Moorcock songs, such as Sonic Attack, Kings Of Speed and Sleep Of A Thousand Tears. His most recent contribution was in 2000, when he appeared 'electronically' with the band as they performed live on stage. This concert is available on a CD called *Yule Ritual.*

Moorcock also wrote lyrics for heavy rock band Blue Öyster Cult and Moorcock's novel *The Fireclown* (aka *The Winds of Limbo*) inspired Pink Floyd's Set The Controls For The Heart Of The Sun. There are further rock music connections: Deep Purple named an album *Stormbringer* after the Elric novel; Diamond Head paid homage to Elric on their *Living On Borrowed Time* album; and the metal bands the Tygers of Pan Tang and Mourneblade took their names from Moorcock books. Moorcock enjoys telling the anecdote of how he taught one friend to play his first three guitar chords and how that friend, Peter Green, went on to co-found Fleetwood Mac.

Moorcock's own band, the Deep Fix, are named after one of his early stories and mentioned in the Jerry Cornelius novels, as well as in *King of the City*. Moorcock and the Deep Fix cut the album *New World's Fair* in 1975, which was reissued on CD in 1995 (then also extended and renamed *Roller Coaster Holiday* in 2006). Deep Fix also recorded the cassette, *The Brothel in Rosenstrasse* (1992) to go with the Moorcock novel of the same name. *The Entropy Tango* was planned as a novel and rock album tie-in, while *Gloriana* nearly became a musical. In 2008, *The Entropy Tango and Gloriana Demo Sessions* was released, and a couple of those tracks found their way onto a Spirits Burning CD. Moorcock even has his own entry in Tony Jasper's *The International Encyclopaedia of Hard Rock and Heavy Metal*.

These were Michael Moorcock's golden years: 'By the mid-1970s I was riding pretty high. My books were selling well. I had won some prizes. Hawkwind… had a platinum disc and we were playing major venues… I edited a magazine, *New Worlds*, which had received notoriety and praise. I was something of a hero of the counterculture… Fame had come easily to me. The attention didn't do much for my character and ultimately led to the breakdown of my first marriage. I was disgustingly self-involved.' He continues to be honest in his self-assessments, owning up that: 'There are some days, however, when reason and humanity desert me completely. I become a monster of egomania, self-pity, psychosomnia, vicious complaint and paranoia.' Famously prolific, this was the time in his life he describes as 'my period of crazed activity when I used to say that if a book took more than three days to write then it wasn't worth writing.'

Nineteen-seventy-eight saw the publication of the sumptuous stand-alone novel, *Gloriana,* and since then Moorcock has tended to write less heroic fantasy and shown more interest in fantastic realism, with the Colonel Pyat novels and the critically acclaimed *Mother London.* He has returned to the Elric mythos, most notably in 1991 with *The Revenge of the Rose,* followed in 2001 by *The Dreamthief's Daughter*, which began a new Elric/von Bek trilogy.

After two failed marriages, Moorcock met his third wife in America. His flirtation with Hollywood and overcoming a near breakdown is poignantly documented in *Letters from Hollywood* (1986), where he finds himself trapped as 'a true serf of a minor movie baron', slowly losing all self-respect. This downward spiral came after escaping bankruptcy and a broken marriage back in England, but his saviour was Linda Steele, who became his wife and with whom he has lived in Austin, Texas, since 1994. Moorcock's sardonic wit ripples through the diaries from America as he describes himself hassled by 'ex-wives telling me they're worried about the rent'. He agrees to send them some money on the condition that they 'consider the possibility of earning some themselves'.

The 1990s saw a revival in the UK of Moorcock's extensive canon with most of his novels and short stories enjoying revision and republication in omnibus form. Millennium/Orion collected his backlist with the aim of linking together his work to create a coherent inter-connectedness to this literary multiverse. Unfortunately, long-term poor health has slowed down his work-rate somewhat. But his books continue to be repackaged and reissued.

Moorcock has gone back to his own childhood heroes of pirates, highwaymen and the Wild West, particularly in *Tales from the Texas Woods* (1997), which includes a 'lost' Sherlock Holmes story.

He even resurrects characters from his teenage years in comic strip writing: most notably *Zenith the Albino* and *Sir Sexton Begg*, a version of that famous London detective, Sexton Blake.

In interviews he often talks about his own talent for structuring novels and seeing the outline and forms before all else, and this is possibly his greatest strength. *Death Is No Obstacle*, a book of interviews with writer Colin Greenland, details his obsession with structure and Moorcock attempts to outline his sense of vision and style. He bases his structures on those constructions, moods and changes used by classical composers, such as Mozart, who Moorcock greatly admires.

As we have established, the range of Moorcock's fiction is enormous and it is easy to forget other avenues, such as his extensive journalism, travel-writing and vociferous political support for anarchism and feminism. Moorcock also co-wrote the screenplay for the film, *The Land That Time Forgot*, and has been involved in developing an interactive computer game called *Silverheart,* based on the 2000 novel co-written with the popular British novelist Storm Constantine. Talk continues of an Elric movie.

He finally completed a trilogy combining Elric and the von Beks in 2004, which possibly completes the entire *Eternal Champion* cycle. In 2006 came the publication of *The Vengeance of Rome*, a book that proved difficult to complete. Since then Moorcock has forayed into the shared-world of Doctor Who books with his contribution, *Coming of the Terraphiles*, drawing on his own multiverse. A new trilogy is to be published, at the end of 2014, with *The Whispering Swarm* — book one of *The Sanctuary of the White Friars*.

Moorcock has embraced the internet as a place where he can communicate with his readers and he spends a great deal of time interacting with the public on a Q&A website (www.multiverse. org). His responses to questions are at times extensive and he has always been generous in the time he gives back to his fans and critics. Whether we can believe every word about the myth which has evolved around Michael Moorcock is debateable, but he has on many occasions described himself simply as an old-fashioned hippy who believes in love, peace and individual liberty. That he has become a cultural icon is beyond doubt.

In a career spanning more than fifty years, Moorcock has always innovated and adhered to the principles laid down in his editorial work for *New Worlds*. Through it Moorcock became known as the editor who inspired the new wave of science fiction in the 1960s. But it is also important to remember that he has also achieved so much more through his own writing. His real legacy is plain for anyone to see, inspiring innumerable writers who have made public the debt they owe to Moorcock, most notable of these being William Gibson, David Gemmell, Kim Newman, Neil Gaiman and Terry Pratchett.

Moorcock now expresses the ideals of a humanist, liberal and freethinking elder statesman. He writes authoritatively about London, city-life, European and US politics, and literature (particularly nineteenth century European fiction), while defiantly championing friends whose own work is often misunderstood or underrated — notably feminist Andrea Dworkin and writers Mervyn Peake and JG Ballard (none of whom are any longer with us). For his original fiction and his influence on modern literature, Moorcock deserves a more recognised place in British literary history.

2: BRAVE NEW WORLDS
'I DON'T BELIEVE THAT ANY TECHNIQUE OR METHOD IS MORE OR LESS USEFUL THAN ANOTHER — EVERYTHING DEPENDS UPON HUMAN TALENT IN THE END.'

Some of Moorcock's early novels used science fiction settings and imagery, but as noted his main impact in the SF field was as editor of *New Worlds* magazine, which became the flagship for the so-called new wave of Science Fiction in the sixties and seventies. Here, Moorcock helped change the definitions of SF; his influence on the genre is an accepted part of the genre's history and the rise of the new wave became focused around the magazine, which attracted writers from Britain and America. Moorcock had had enough of formula SF, with its sexist obsessions and preponderance of war against 'bug-eyed monsters', and he chose *New Worlds* as a focus because it seemed most open to new ideas.

New Worlds began in 1936 as a fanzine *Novae Terrae*, and was published professionally in 1946 when taken over by John Carnell (known to his friends as Ted). It became the leading British publication of its type, preferring what we would now call classic SF at the higher quality end of the genre, rather than the poorer standard found in the pulp magazines. This was what originally attracted Moorcock to *New Worlds*. Carnell accepted stories by Arthur C Clarke, John Brunner and John Wyndham. The latter's 'For All the Night' followed the adventures of a space travelling family. Also published in the fifties was 'The Streets of Ashkelon' by Harry Harrison, about a priest and atheist on another planet. Most of the fiction fell under the typical themes and trappings of SF: life in space; time travel; future wars and technology; battles with aliens.

In the March 1963 issue of *New Worlds Science Fiction* (vol. 43, no. 128) Moorcock wrote a letter in response to John Baxter's editorial some issues previous, in which he agrees that 'SF writers have become perhaps too parochial in outlook'. He mentions Brian Aldiss as an exemplary writer, then groups Aldiss with Samuel Beckett, William Golding and Iris Murdoch. He bemoans how science fiction merely produces 'an abortive aping of mainstream experimentation' with flat characters and no real plot. This is, Moorcock argues, 'the lazy writer's dream', leading only to 'hollow derivative stuff'. By referring to non science fiction texts, Moorcock challenges genre writers to compete with literary authors and not to be satisfied with 'almost-good'. However, this improvement in literature, Moorcock adds, will come about 'by evolution rather than revolution'.

On the strength of this, editor John Carnell invited young Moorcock to do a guest editorial in the April 1963 issue (vol. 43, no. 129). His essay, entitled 'Play with Feeling', is a lengthy rant about the state of science fiction and his hopes for the future of British writing. He admits: 'SF is one of the most potentially flexible media for the presentation of the human drama there has been', but then argues that this potential has yet to be seized upon. He expresses a hope that 'as science fiction grows up... it will produce as many variations as there are in ordinary fiction'. While this has in part has come about, SF is still somewhat marginalized by critics.

Moorcock comments on how science fiction 'is essentially a romantic medium' which should be dealing with proper literary tropes, such as irony and satire, even citing Shakespeare and Brecht as standards. A list of what he considers to be lacking from writers is a long and damning one: 'passion, subtlety, irony, original characterisation, original and good style, a sense of involvement in human affairs, colour, density, depth and, on the whole, real feeling from the writer.' After a swift discussion of Romanticism and a further plea for 'richer' plots and characters, Moorcock's tone becomes visionary: 'It is my contention that a mixture of the fabulous and the familiar can produce art which comes closer to defining Truth than anything else'. Thus succinctly describing his own writing.

Moorcock had a vision for 'a different kind of fiction [which] could come out of a marriage between experimental forms and old-style genre SF'. Bored with the modernist novels of the fifties and sixties exemplified by Kingsley Amis, Moorcock became ambitious and with the help of JG Ballard began an experiment in form, narrative and language. *New Worlds* did more than revolutionise SF; it encouraged and nurtured a completely new direction in contemporary fiction. Moorcock was at pains to explain his use of terms, such as science fiction, much preferring 'science fantasy'. Rather than choose stories because they fitted a generic pattern, Moorcock selected anything original and inventively subversive, always keen to break down barriers and generic conventions.

A year later, Moorcock took the full-time editorial seat of the revamped journal, *New Worlds SF*. His vision of science fiction as stylish, experimental literature full of 'passion and craftsmanship' set the template for what he sought for his new magazine. By including stories from JG Ballard and Brian Aldiss, plus an essay about William Burroughs, Moorcock set out his intentions immediately with *New Worlds* dated May-June 1964 (vol. 48, no. 142). His editorial, 'A New Literature for the Space Age,' also discusses William Burroughs' exciting, experimental, controversial prose, which 'uses advanced and effective literary techniques'. (Moorcock defended Burroughs in the famous *Times Literary Supplement* 'UGH!' correspondence around the same time, after the *TLS* wrote a damning review of *Dead Fingers*

Talk. Moorcock was one of many literary figures who spoke out for Burroughs in what became a heated controversy in artistic circles.) In *New Worlds*, Moorcock urged readers to dismiss 'the fast-stagnating pool of the conventional novel' and to turn to what he calls 'speculative fantasy'. Burroughs employs imagery that is both 'stimulating and thought-provoking'; Moorcock calls for other writers to follow this example by 'producing a kind of SF which is unconventional in every sense and which must soon be recognised as an important revitalisation of the literary mainstream'. Then Moorcock intensifies his tone into a rallying cry: 'This is a sign... that a popular literary renaissance is around the corner.'

For the issue dated March 1965 (vol. 48, no. 148), Moorcock broadened the scope of the magazine. While he had doubled the magazine's circulation and published a wide variety of writers and writing, the editor kept a consistent approach to his definition of SF, having identified a particular problem: 'We need more writers who reflect the pragmatic mood of today, who use images apt for today... a writer must write primarily for his own generation... He can learn from his predecessors, but he should not imitate them'. The definition is further refined later that year (vol. 49, no. 152) with Moorcock's emphasis on the rejection of what he called 'popular engineering articles thinly disguised as fiction'.

By September 1966 (vol. 50, no. 166) it felt like the experiment had worked, as Moorcock suggests in his essay, 'Why So Conservative?' In fact the success meant that it now faced stiff competition from outside the genre: 'What we choose to call the "mainstream" is doing almost everything that SF was doing ten or twenty years ago — and it is doing it better than SF was doing it then!' Moorcock gravely warns that if science fiction doesn't compete with mainstream fiction then it 'will remain what it was until fairly recently — the fat, intelligent, often sardonic, colourfully-dressed eunuch of literature'.

Through his courageous editorial policy and his risky support of new talent, Moorcock single-handedly created this new form of speculative fiction, which became more concerned with man's alienation from the world, expressed through imagery rooted in the modern world and relevant to popular culture. As Moorcock wrote in the 1968 editorial of *Best SF Stories from New Worlds 3*: 'Through their fiction *New Worlds* writers are... pioneers to the new, strange countries of the mind which will exist tomorrow. They have not lost their sense of wonder... They are providing us with information, a language, a code, a new mythology... as they continue the exploration of the interior.' He considered *New Worlds* to be an avant-garde literary journal rather than a science fiction magazine.

The inspiration for this new mode of fiction came from pioneers as diverse as artist Salvador Dalì, whose paintings expressed a feeling of dilapidation and ennui; writer William Burroughs, whose fragmented writing explored human consciousness heightened by drugs (leading to paranoia and other altered states); psychologist Carl Jung, whose studies of myth and ritual were closely linked to imagination and spirituality; and rock hero Jimi Hendrix, the virtuoso guitarist who stretched the boundaries of youth culture by preaching free sex and the use of drugs. The new territory to be explored became known as 'inner-space', a concept introduced by JG Ballard in *New Worlds Science Fiction* issue 118, which implies an existentialist condition that explores real life experiences such as alienation, sexuality, drug trips and psychosis. Moorcock was obsessed with the ambition to celebrate inventive, radical and relevant writing, which would go beyond the limited genre of science fiction and cross over into literary and, more importantly, popular culture.

JG Ballard's subsequent world-renowned success is mostly due to Moorcock's tenacity and faith in his early experiments. Ballard had only positive comments to make about his friend: 'Mike was a great editor and *New Worlds* under his editorship was the most important literary magazine of the sixties.' Another contributor and critic, John Clute, said that while Moorcock was full of 'elated youthfulness', *New Worlds* was nevertheless an important 'nutrient tank' adding a rich texture to a confused sixties culture. While not all the stories were wholly successful, the magazine was clearly a catalyst for a paradigm shift in science fiction.

The new wave occurred in London in the early sixties with Moorcock encouraging the popularity of arts like rock music, comics and fine art, and there was a link between *New Worlds* and the infamous underground magazines *Frendz, Oz* and *International Times.* Moorcock printed the writing and artwork of Mervyn Peake, the poetry of George MacBeth and published *Entropy* by Thomas Pynchon for the first time in England. It was also *New Worlds* that introduced the art of MC Escher to Britain in 1967. Regular contributors included authors now respected in their own right: Ballard, Brian Aldiss, DM Thomas, Thomas M Disch, John Brunner, M John Harrison, Samuel R Delany, Gene Wolfe, Harry Harrison, Robert Silverberg, Christopher Priest and Robert Holdstock. Terry Pratchett's first story, 'Night Dweller' was featured in 1965 and Moorcock accepted an early story by William Gibson. In its changing fortunes over a decade, *New Worlds* received an Arts Council grant, but the magazine was also banned by book chain WHSmith's and mentioned in Parliament for the salacious content of one story, 'Bug Jack Barron' by Norman Spinrad, before it became a well-known novel.

In his study of science fiction writers, *Science Fiction: Ten Explorations*, literary scholar CN Manlowe interpreted the new wave in the following way: '*New Worlds* under the editorship of Michael Moorcock aimed to break down the genre fence of science fiction and while still retaining its imaginative and technical licence with reality, make it capable of effects which would give it authority as literature in its own right.'

Contributor and later editor, Charles Platt explains in his book on SF and fantasy writers, *Dreammakers*, how Moorcock sustained much of the momentum: 'He was iconoclastic and flamboyant. He became the editorial focus for new writing talent... There was a sense of significance and destiny about the whole thing.'

It seems that the development of SF itself owes much to what Brian Aldiss calls 'the Moorcockian revolution'. Moorcock with his radical *New Worlds* editorial policy subverted traditional SF expectations, believing instead, he wrote in one issue (vol. 49, no. 151), that: 'SF is simply imaginative fiction. It is speculative about science, religion, art, anything treated in a fresh and imaginative way... The emphasis can be psychological, sociological, metaphysical, the treatment can be surrealistic, realistic or deliberately extravagant.'

New Worlds: an Anthology appeared in 1983 with a lengthy introduction by Moorcock. He described the fertile period between 1964-1971 as 'an ambience... a revolutionary and stimulating period'. He concludes that 'it is anger, impatience, optimism and idealism, not nostalgia of any sort, which creates the most worthwhile and lasting changes'.

With the value of hindsight, Moorcock reflected in 1991 (*NW* vol.62, no 217) how 'Literary SF has never been more central to common experience, never more valid and rarely better..."the mainstream" is today little more than one exhausted tributary of the literary flood'. This assertion suggests that the new wave experiments he spearheaded in the sixties and seventies had the desired effect of bringing experimental fiction to the forefront and up to the standard of the mainstream. In 2011 (in his introduction written for online magazine paraxis.org), Moorcock summed up the results of his experiment by stating 'Literary visionary fiction is now the form of fiction best positioned to take us into the next decades of the century'.

While the experiments were championed by some and at the same time came under great criticism from other quarters, Moorcock continued to emphasise the importance of the magazine. Looking back, he has commented that *'New Worlds...* was not merely its graphics, its articles, its controversies, or, indeed, its fiction. It was an ambience... a revolutionary and stimulating period.' Fantasy and science fiction have never quite been the same since.

Moorcock's own stories were some of the most original and experimental. He began by writing with Barrington Bayley, but soon developed his own individual style. Once installed as editor he took to using pseudonyms for his own contributions, the most common being James Colvin and William Barclay.

Instead of referring to the universe, Moorcock coined the term 'multiverse' to describe the overlapping alternate worlds and realities that his characters inhabit. The concept was introduced in the 1962 story 'Sundered Worlds', published in *Science Fiction Adventures* magazine (the story also became a novel, published both as *The Sundered Worlds* and *The Blood Red Game*) to describe multiple universes and planes of existence, which run concurrently and where alternative times and realities co-exist and occasionally interact. The protagonist, Renark, explains the theory of the multiverse as 'the multi-dimensional universe containing dozens of different universes, separated from each other by unknown dimensions'.

Moorcock himself defined his multiverse as a 'near-infinite nest of universes, each only marginally different from the next... where "rogue" universes can take sideways orbits, crashing through the dimensions and creating all kinds of disruptions in the delicate fabric of multiversal space-time'. Sometimes the planes and times intersect, and various characters, such as Edwardian traveller Oswald Bastable, join the League of Temporal Adventurers who have learned to travel across time and space.

'The Time Dweller' (1964) appeared in *New Worlds* before Moorcock became its editor and it tells how the Scar-faced Brooder learns how to manipulate time so that he can shift between planes or 'time-streams'. This is an important concept in many later Moorcock novels, not least the Jerry Cornelius series and Oswald Bastable trilogy. In a follow up story, 'Escape from Evening' (1965), we learn more about the Time Dwellers who are 'capable of moving through time as others move through space'. The central time stream through our own universe is called the 'megaflow'.

Moorcock's use of alternate worlds began in the story 'The Pleasure Garden of Felipe Sagittarius' (1965). This presents readers with a version of earth in which Hitler is a captain in the Berlin police working under Bismarck, and Einstein is 'an embittered old mathematics teacher'. Moorcock continues to be keen to portray 'the infinity of possible realities, each subtly different, which exist throughout the multiverse, that decidedly non-linear celebration of our own marvellous minds'.

The richest example of Jungian fiction in *New Worlds* came in the story, 'The Golden Barge'. (It was an unpublished novel in 1957, condensed into a short story in 1965, and finally published as a novel in 1979.) The narrative, which has an elusive dream-like quality that owes something to Mervyn Peake, presents Jephraim Tallow distracted from his destiny to follow the mysterious and eponymous barge. He is tempted away by a woman whose love seems perfect until he is driven to kill her. In this exploration of sexuality and human motivation, Moorcock employs ornate language and dense psychological symbolism that makes his writing stand above much else that was written at the time: 'Tears painted his face in gleaming trails, he was breathing quickly, his brain in a tumult, a dozen emotions clashing together, making him powerless for any action save speech. He gave in suddenly, ashamed for her degradation. He sank down beside her, taking her wet, heaving body in his arms and in sympathy with her grief. And so, locked together in their fear and their bewilderment, they slept.'

'The Deep Fix' (1963) was published in *New World*'s sister magazine *Science Fantasy*, and is an important contribution to a subgenre of fiction that explores altered states of consciousness. A research scientist named Seward uses hallucinogenic drugs to travel inside his own mind to discover a formula that will save the sanity of the earth's population. Moorcock considered this to be a key story, naming his own rock band after it. It also links Moorcock with American writers such as William Burroughs and Philip K Dick, who were also openly discussing the use of drugs and their effects upon human perception. 'The Deep Fix' interrogates the infinite conundrum regarding dreams, fantasy and reality by asking the essential question; who knows what is real?

If the two main themes of *New Worlds* were psychology and sexuality then nowhere was this more compellingly explored than in Moorcock's story, 'Behold the Man' (1966), which was developed into a novel in 1969. While the short story is powerful, the novel expands the ideas even further and is worth examining as a significant result of the new wave experiment. *Behold the Man* subverts the Christian salvation story by casting an ordinary, flawed mortal in the role of Christ. It is a disturbing expression of Moorcock's mistrust of religious authority.

The protagonist of *Behold the Man* is Karl Glogauer, a twentieth century Jew whose fantasies confuse religious icons with sexual obsessions. Throughout the novel, Glogauer's mind becomes as fragmented as the text itself. After discovering that 'time is nothing to do with space — it is to do with the psyche' he chooses to go back in time to meet Jesus Christ. Glogauer is at first forced to reject his own identity and take on the mantle of the Messiah himself, after being shocked at discovering that Jesus of Nazareth is merely a gibbering imbecile. In a schizophrenic passion 'Karl Glogauer entered Christ and Christ entered Jerusalem'. Acting out the role he begins to enjoy the self-importance of becoming Saviour of Mankind and Glogauer's motive is a very real need for some kind of personal identity.

The text is made up of dual narratives, jumping from earlier memories of sexual and intellectual frustrations to his arrival in Jerusalem. The irony becomes more complex and involved as we hear Glogauer in the twentieth century debating the existence of Christ and stating: 'I'm not a martyr.' Yet it seems to be his destiny. As he takes on the messiahship, he remembers the future — a twentieth century in which his psychologist girlfriend, Monica, had left him a note with the words, 'Christianity is just a new name for a conglomeration of old myths and philosophies. All the Gospels do is retell the sun myth and garble some ideas from the Greeks and Romans.' He is unaware that he too will continue the cycle, once more reinventing the 'messiah myth'.

In a discussion with Monica, Glogauer states: 'Jung knew that the myth can also create the reality.' The question being asked is — does it matter if the death and resurrection of Christ are true or is it the symbolism that is relevant? In this respect, Karl Glogauer has both created the myth and been drawn into it, because he believed that humanity needed it to be true. He took the responsibility, or at least indulged in the power it would bring, on the understanding that a counterfeit Christ was better than no Christ at all. At least the myth would be there for people to put their faith in and perhaps faith in a myth is preferable to having no hope at all. The symbolism of the cross and resurrection eventually transcends its own historical veracity.

Glogauer is himself an amateur psychologist and he realises that he can cure hysterical symptoms and neuroses, showing how twentieth century understanding of medicine and illness has led to different conclusions and interpretations of what were once considered miracles. Psychology, it seems, has become the new religion, or at least, the theology of postmodern society, and Moorcock offers a psychological interpretation of spiritual healing: 'Many he could do nothing for, but others, obviously with remediable psychosomatic conditions, he could help. They believed in his power more strongly than they believed in their sickness. So he cured them.'

His radical psychological framework is an exploration and realisation of the existential beliefs that theologian Don Cupitt calls modern Western Christians to in his book, *The Sea of Faith*: 'This task of working out a vision of God takes the more human and concrete form of framing a personal vision of Christ, who is our own ideal alter ego, our true Self that we are to become our religious ideal actualised in human form.'

Glogauer in *Behold the Man* lives out this self-realisation and offers the extreme example. This does suggest that we create our own gods, demons and heroes; our own hopes and despairs; our own law and chaos. Moorcock remains optimistic and hopeful with his agnostic belief that love conquers death.

The stark ending of *Behold the Man* offers no answers or solutions and the novel avoids didacticism, preferring to ask questions. The character of Glogauer is a bigot and not a sympathetic character. Moorcock had a challenging aim, which he explains in *Death Is No Obstacle*: 'I hope to suggest to the reader that we all share some responsibility for the world's ills... Glogauer is something of a victim and product of his society, but it doesn't excuse anything he does.'

THE LAW OF CHAOS

The themes of fate, time, psychology and sexuality explored in *New Worlds* were developed further in Moorcock's works that have become collectively known as *The Tale of the Eternal Champion*. Through this interconnected series of novels, trilogies and tetralogies Moorcock expounds his philosophical dualism of law and chaos and expands his concept of what he termed the multiverse. Closely related to his concept of the multiverse is that of the *Eternal Champion*.

3: THE ETERNAL CHAMPION

'I HAVE DIFFICULTY DEFINING "FANTASY" AS A READILY DEFINABLE GENRE — OR FREQUENTLY EVEN AS AN ELEMENT.'

The Eternal Champion is the generic name for all the incarnations of the one hero who appears in different novels, in different times and places, in various guises throughout the multiverse. Within the entire cycle of novels, known collectively as *The Tale of the Eternal Champion*, Moorcock's different characters, themes, settings and plots overlap through a conscious internal-referencing and intertextuality. Moorcock's fantasies are all interconnected through the various avatars of the Eternal Champion: an everyman hero who fights either chaos or law on behalf of humanity. The best known are those from his sword and sorcery fantasies — Elric the albino; Erekosë the immortal; Corum, the prince in the scarlet robe; Hawkmoon with the jewel in his skull — although the term also applies to Jerry Cornelius, von Bek, Oswald Bastable and so many others.

Moorcock in his early heroic fantasies shows a great preference for romantic protagonists, such as Elric, sometimes called the Womanslayer, a tragic hero akin to Charles Maturin's *Melmoth the Wanderer* and Lord Byron's *Manfred*. Elric fits the template of the gothic romantic character type — the demon-lover. The albino prince of Melniboné first appeared in the 1961 story, 'The Dreaming City' in *Science Fantasy* magazine and owed something to Anthony Skene's character, Zenith the Albino. Elric is dependent at first upon drugs and herbs for strength, then later upon a sinister chaos sword, Stormbringer, which being both sentient and vampiric, thirsts for blood and for the souls of any living creature. This acts as a symbiotic relationship in which

Elric becomes bloodthirsty in exchange for physical energy. He is a tortured and neurotic character struggling with pain, anxiety and tragedy after killing his lover, Cymoril. Elric is the inversion of the hero archetype: flawed and therefore, ironically, extremely human.

As a homeless mercenary, Elric pursues a number of supernatural quests, evoking elemental spirits, riding dragons and working for Arioch, a god of chaos. On many of his adventures he is joined by the enigmatic character, Moonglum, the eternal companion.

Elric's destiny is to bring balance to a world in which the gods of Chaos and Law are in constant conflict. In the story, 'While the Gods Laugh' (1961) Elric expresses the following paradox: 'The upholders of Chaos state that in such a world as they rule all things are possible. Opponents of Chaos... say that without Law nothing material is possible.' Before he dies in the novel *Stormbringer* (1965), Elric sees that the world ruled by Law is no different to that ruled by Chaos. After asking Sepiriz (an immortal servant of Fate) the meaning of the cosmic balance, an ambiguous answer is returned: "Who can know why the Cosmic Balance exists, why Fate exists and the Lords of the Higher Worlds? There seems to be an infinity of space and time and possibilities... Perhaps all is cyclic and this same event will occur again and again until the universe is run down and fades away... Meaning, Elric? Do not seek that, for madness lies in such a course.' Elric, the Eternal Champion, finally discovers a purpose for living and a reason for his frailty, for it is only in our weakness and sense of the finite that we can have true freedom.

In *Stormbringer* his destiny is revealed explicitly in a vivid dream: 'And the cycles turn and spin and intersect at unpredictable points in an eternity of possibilities, paradoxes and conjunctions... Thus we influence past, present and future and all their possibilities.

Thus are we all responsible for one another ...' The Elric novels are full of such philosophical introspection interspersed with violent action. The plots follow epic style quests and usually end with a large-scale battle and resolution.

Many of the early Eternal Champion stories were very personal. Moorcock explains today that: 'Elric was me (the me of 1960-1, anyway) and the mingled qualities of betrayer and betrayed, the bewilderment about life in general, the search for some solution to it all, the expression of this bewilderment in terms of violence, cynicism and the need for revenge, were all mine.' The alienated hero reflected the inner quest of Moorcock himself, who admits to using personal symbolism within the text to express his own obsessions. Certainly, Elric is the character with whom the writer most closely identifies and Moorcock admits to early and youthful attempts at self-dramatization, wish-fulfilment and catharsis through these fantasy novels.

The material, external multiverse is a projection of the chaos of our own psyche or id. Moorcock believes that, 'When we read a good fantasy we are being admitted into the subterranean worlds of our own souls.' His *Eternal Champion* novels are charged with personal and metaphysical symbolism.

Erekosë was introduced in the first book Moorcock planned to write, *The Eternal Champion* (written in 1957, first published as a novella in 1962), which acts as the opening of *The Tale of the Eternal Champion* cycle and is probably influenced by Norse and Icelandic myths. The protagonist begins as John Daker in the twentieth century, but has to learn a new identity as Erekosë, a demi-god, cursed to always be aware that he is more than one person and in visions sees his other avatars. Erekosë is the most unfortunate as he is the one who can see his own destiny and feel the pain of every incarnation. He is pulled through time and space to enter an eternal cycle and never know peace. In the revised version of *The Eternal Champion* (Millennium 1992) Moorcock added the names of other champions to develop the interconnections: 'Was I John Daker or Erekosë? Was I either of these? Many other names — Corum Jhaelen Irsei, Aubec, Sexton Begg, Elric, Rackhir, Ilian, Oona, Simon, Bastable, Cornelius, The Rose, von Bek, Asquiol, Hawkmoon — fled away down the ghostly rivers of my memory.' The author states that the book 'forms the chief rationale and central metaphor to my fiction' and acts as the key to all his heroic fantasy writing.

The most tormented of the champions, Erekosë, expresses this truth when he claims the right to be 'free to be the flawed, finite, mortal creatures which from the first was all we ever wished to be'. The cycle turns and keeps turning. It is up to the Eternal Champion to make sure the balance is kept in equilibrium lest the world should suffer the legalistic, stifling tyranny of law, or the anarchic insanity of chaos.

Erekosë is conscious of his powerlessness over the destiny that controls him and is doomed to never know his true identity. In *Phoenix in Obsidian* (1970), he becomes Urlik Skarsol with a black sword that has similarities to Elric's Stormbringer, and then *The Dragon in the Sword* (1986, and a precursor to *The Dreamthief's Daughter*) sees London-born John Daker confronting Hitler in an alternate earth history in which the Nazis become agents of chaos, and Daker and Ulrich von Bek find the Holy Grail. The alternate worlds in these novels are examples of Moorcock's multiverse. The Erekosë novels are written in first person, which make them stand out, and they are the most introspective of Moorcock's heroic fantasies, expressing the anguished thoughts of someone attempting to discover his own identity in a complex world.

Corum comes from the old world of Cornish mythology and his castle at Moidel's Mount is based on St. Michael's Mount near Penzance, which is linked with Arthurian legends. He is an elfin aesthete who desires peace and contentment, but who only learns anger and revenge from the humans, or 'mabden', who disrupt his life with their hatred and malice. Corum learns that his destiny is to fight for equilibrium and he vanquishes the gods of chaos, Arioch, Xiombarg and Mabelode. He also meets Elric and Erekosë who help to rescue his companion, Jhary-a-Conel, from the Vanishing Tower. At the end of the first Corum trilogy in *The King of the Swords* (1972), all the gods of chaos and law are killed and banished leaving an existential utopia where individuals create their own destinies — a state of *deus absconditus*.

The second trilogy parallels Corum with the Celtic hero Cuchulain, so beloved by WB Yeats. Corum has supernatural powers when his eye and hand are prosthetically transplanted by the eye and hand of twin gods that enable him to see into limbo and call the damned to his aid in his struggle against Prince Gaynor. Explicit references are made to druids and the Sidhe, thus showing that Moorcock was influenced by the Celtic mythologies.

The name Corum Jhaelen Irsei is an anagram of Jeremiah Cornelius, another of Moorcock's eternal champions, from which is also derived Jherek Carnelian and Jhary-a-Conel. He contrives to use many names with the initials J.C., which perhaps links his protagonists with the ultimate everyman, Jesus Christ.

Hawkmoon is another gothic romantic hero, being a prisoner of war, initially controlled by the enemy but eventually awakening to individuality. The balance is symbolised by the talismanic Runestaff and is served by the mysterious Warrior in Jet and Gold, a character whose motives and status are ambiguous and who also appears in the Corum novels. He works for fate, like Sepiriz in the Elric mythos.

The first four novels, beginning with *The Jewel in the Skull* (1967) and known as *The History of the Runestaff*, explain how Hawkmoon is controlled by a jewel and how he fights the evil empire of Granbretan, aided by the mysterious supernatural powers of the Runestaff. The Hawkmoon books are perhaps the most stark and barbaric of Moorcock's fantasies. It becomes clear that this is Europe in a post-apocalyptic, primitive future and, ironically, London (Londra) has become an anarchic city of savages set against a German hero. The books are full of vivid descriptions of pagan rituals, futuristic flying machines and the memorable Emperor who is a foetus enthroned in a womb-like globe.

There are games for the reader to play and much fun can be had spotting the bastardised names of real places, such as Kroiden (Croydon), and names of famous British twentieth century politicians, such as 'Chirshil... and Aral Vilsn' (Churchill and Harold Wilson). There are even references to some of his own friends, such as JG Ballard and Brian Aldiss, and also to the Beatles: 'Gilded figureheads decorated the forward parts of the ships, representing the terrifying ancient gods of Granbretan — *Jhone, Jhorg, Phowl, Rhunga.*'

The final three Hawkmoon books are referred to as The Chronicles of Castle Brass and they conclude the entire complex Tale of the Eternal Champion cycle. *Count Brass* recounts the defence of Castle Brass in a medieval alternate France, a land of hope and romance. In *The Champion of Garathorm*, Hawkmoon turns into Queen Ilian, a heroine at last.

In the final novel *The Quest for Tanelorn* Elric, Erekose, Corum and Hawkmoon physically unite to make a creature called The Four Who Were One and in this guise, the Eternal Champion experiences a moment akin to enlightenment when he confronts the entire multiverse and knows no fear: 'For the mind of man alone is free to explore the lofty vastness of the cosmic infinite, to transcend ordinary consciousness, or roam the subterranean corridors of the human brain with its boundless dimensions. And the universe and individual are linked, the one mirrored in the other, and each contains the other.' This episode is echoed in the Elric novel, *The Sailor On the Seas of Fate*, which cleverly tells the same story, but from Elric's viewpoint.

Tanelorn is Moorcock's equivalent to the Elysian Fields of Greek mythology or King Arthur's Avalon, where even the Eternal Champion might find peace. Tanelorn has the ability to shift between planes and protect itself from the outside threats of law or chaos. In the final chapter of the *Eternal Champion* cycle, in the novel *The Quest for Tanelorn* (1975), there occurs the Conjunction of a Million Spheres in which all the champions meet in the city, guided by a child called Jehamiah Cohnahlias (another derived name). A final apocalyptic vision helps explain much of the fantastical symbolism, and it becomes clear what the chaos sword of Elric, Stormbringer, and the black jewel of Hawkmoon, represent, as both transform into one dark figure: 'John ap-Rhyss said calmly, "In Yel, in the villages, they have a legend of such a creature. Say-tunn, is that his name?" The child shrugged. "Give him any name and he grows in power. Refuse him a name and his power weakens. I call him Fear. Mankind's greatest enemy."' This had been hinted at in the final paragraph of *Stormbringer*, which is repeated here as Hawkmoon's dream.

The sword and sorcery novels always depict the multiversal struggle between the powers of chaos and law and this dualism is a struggle that must be reconciled to achieve individual, creative or cosmic balance. The scales of balance between chaos and order become a political and even religious symbol in many of Moorcock's fantasy works, and love can only be achieved when the two are in equilibrium.

For Moorcock, 'law' is a representation of reason, the rational, logical side of human nature with its preference for order, facts and organisation; namely utilitarianism. Chaos, on the other hand, is a symbol for human emotion, something akin to romance, which can be associated with mythology, the imagination, or in psychological terms, with the unconscious. Romance is a literature of feelings and sensibilities that allows the existence of the supernatural, such as the great gothic romances of the eighteenth century. Romance is often seen as a form opposed to realism or mimetic fiction.

Moorcock freely admits to purloining some of the imagery of the cosmic struggle from Poul Anderson's fantasy novel *Three Hearts and Three Lions* (1953). In a 1963 essay Moorcock explained his cosmology by including a 'Cosmic Hand' at the top of the chain — above gods, elementals, sorcerers, men and beasts. It is up to people to fight to maintain a balance.

The dualism of order and chaos is far more complicated than the traditional dualism of good and evil, which is more simplistic. Moorcock explained in an interview with *Vector*, the critical journal of the British Science Fiction Association, that 'Law and Chaos are both attractive, both dangerous, and both become worthless if you push them too far'. In the justice system, chaos and law are interdependent. Chaos represents the imagination, danger and passion, while law represents science, safety and sterility.

Nietzsche wrote, in *The Birth of Tragedy* (1871), about the tension in Greek tragedy between the wild, chaotic Dionysian urge, which is tempered by the restraint and reason of the Apollonian, and how both are required to Greek Tragedy. Moorcock's use of chaos and law follows the same model. It becomes clear that chaos and law, whether as religious imagery, philosophical concept, literary metaphor or even personal spirituality, are states to keep in balance. Both are necessary components of a dualism, which implies not so much that they are opposites, but complementary halves to a whole, like the combination of the masculine and feminine in us all. This is also further symbolised by the symbol of the hermaphrodite that reappears in several of Moorcock's novels (*The Final Programme*, *The City in the Autumn Stars* or the androgyne in *The Dragon In the Sword*). Balance between the two ideals is the only answer; law is required for communal living but stifles creativity, and chaos inspires art but brings violence and loss of security. Humans need to be emotional and artistic, but if they are to be communal animals then it demands conforming to some consensus.

In Moorcock's sword and sorcery novels spiritual warfare is shown in apocalyptic and surreal visions of worldly battles between creatures and men (most incarnations of the Champion are men, except Ilian of Garathorm and later, the Rose) where, typically, the hordes of chaos are massing for a final confrontation against law. The Eternal Champion fights on whichever side needs help to counteract the flux or entropy (the loss of energy and order) and to create equilibrium. The Cosmic Balance is the overarching power, which controls fate, and the Balance is the closest Moorcock gets to explaining the role or existence of God. It is the cause for which the Eternal Champion is doomed to fight against his will, and this Balance is often represented at the end of a novel by a pair of scales projected upon the heavens. Moorcock suggests that humans are not necessarily fallen or sinful, but are individuals, who are essentially self-responsible, who need rules and routine as well as the chaos of freedom to lead a sane, balanced existence.

Gods, it seems, are merely human metaphors; balance, or fate, is multiversal justice, represented by Sepiriz or the enigmatic Warrior in Jet and Gold. If there are no gods, then all responsibility is left with the individual. When Elric opens The Dead God's Book, which contains the truth about both the balance and the multiverse, it tragically crumbles to dust in his hands. He concludes, 'There is no Truth but that of eternal struggle.' Moorcock, here, investigates the concept of determinism and concludes that fate is merely mythical symbolism. The reader is left sympathising with the Eternal Champion in his quest for meaning and personal identity.

In an essay collected in *Sojan* (1977), Moorcock explained his aims in writing the Elric stories: 'There is... no Holy Grail which will transform a man overnight from bewildered ignorance to complete knowledge — the answer is already within him, if he cares to train himself to find it.'

Most of the novels that comprise The Tale of the Eternal Champion are early Moorcock novels that follow a visionary sequence. They fit into a structured plan to write one gigantic novel and each one has been carefully structured. Moorcock does not, however, wish to be remembered as a writer of sword and sorcery, and he now boasts that many of these books were written quickly. The Hawkmoon books, for example, were each written in three days and he thought nothing of producing 15,000 words a day. In fact, between 1965 and 1975 Moorcock wrote about forty books. The Eternal Champion books were written to a formula, one that he developed and that has been much copied since. The Champions usually embark on a quest for a surrogate Holy Grail, which will bring harmony to the struggle between chaos and law.

Since 1989, however, Moorcock's heroic fantasy novels have been more considered and written in a more literary style, particularly *The Fortress of the Pearl* (1989), which introduces Oone the Dreamthief, and *The Revenge of the Rose* (1991), both books continuing the Elric saga. *The Revenge of the Rose* saw the Rose added to the pantheon, who has since appeared in the *Second Ether* trilogy (beginning with *Blood*, 1994) and *King of the City* (2000). She is the strongest female Eternal Champion and is related to the von Bek family, discussed later (see chapter nine) along with the 2001 novel, *The Dreamthief's Daughter*.

The author has developed a metaphysical cosmology building into a gigantic interconnected mythology. The conscious self-

and cross-referencing of the author is often only a code for the initiated and devoted reader. The same characters appear in different contexts, so Wheldrake the poet can accompany Elric as well as exist in the court of Gloriana. Moorcock wants to see how the same character responds in contrasting situations and ages. Elric becomes al Rikh in *King of the City*, and Count Ulrich von Bek in the forty-two page novella 'The Ghost Warriors' (*Tales from the Texas Woods*, 1997) and in *The Dreamthief's Daughter*.

The Eternal Champion fights the ubiquitous battle of law versus chaos and these fantasy novels raise teleological issues, leaving the reader with the existential conclusion that we are the masters of our own destiny. Moorcock explained it succinctly on his question and answer website: 'If I was God and wanted to make an experiment, I'd set it up pretty much as it is now — and free will would be crucial to the system — because free will invents solutions to problems better than anything else. So if I wanted to make a self-sustaining system, I suppose this is the kind I'd make and non-interference and free will would have to be built into the rules. Therefore I see the world as a self-sustaining organism, at least ideally. It's up to us to make the best of it.'

4: JERRY CORNELIUS
'HE'S EVERYTHING. EVERYONE.'

Jerry Cornelius first appeared in *New Worlds* in 1965 as a fragment of what would eventually become *The Final Programme* (1968), followed by three more novels: *A Cure For Cancer* (1971), *The English Assassin* (1972) and *The Condition of Muzak* (1977). The entire Cornelius sequence is, however, more than the sum of these four volumes and include a number of spin-off novels and innumerable stories — although not all by Moorcock. The 1971 anthology, *The Nature of the Catastrophe*, included stories by Brian Aldiss, M John Harrison and Norman Spinrad. The figure of Jerry Cornelius became an iconic cartoon strip character in the underground magazine *International Times (IT)*, drawn by Mal Dean, with R Glyn Jones as co-artist and written by Moorcock with M John Harrison. Jerry Cornelius reappeared in the 1998 DC comic series *Michael Moorcock's Multiverse*, and in a story, 'The Spencer Inheritance' (*The Edge*, June 1998), referring to the death of Princess Diana. Then in 2011, the character reappeared in *Modem Times 2.0* from PM Press.

With the original four experimental novels, Moorcock managed to capture the zeitgeist of the sixties and seventies through his invocation of street-talk, popular fashion, music, promiscuity and the pop culture. As also a rock musician who writes about music, Moorcock believes that, just as jazz inspired the beat generation, so pop music inspired young British writers like himself. He identified with the hipsters, beatniks and more specifically with the psychedelic hippy movement. Later, his anarchist idealism led to support of the punk movement, and to his writing a Jerry Cornelius novel which tied in with the Sex Pistols film, *The Great Rock'n'Roll Swindle* (1980). Two comic spin-offs, *The Chinese Agent* (aka *Somewhere in the Night*, 1966) and *The Russian Intelligence* (aka *The Printer's Devil*, 1966) are spoof detective novels following the investigations of one Jerry Cornell.

Literary scholar Mikhail Bakhtin writes about popular festive forms in *Rabelais and His World*, when he explains how 'For thousands of years the people have used these festive comic images to express their criticism, their deep distrust of official truth, and their highest hopes and aspirations'. In sixties and seventies England, pop culture became the modern form of carnival and an important form of expression for individual freedom. Moorcock successfully utilised this mood, capturing the spirit of the times. It is this optimistic and rebellious spirit that pervades the entire Jerry Cornelius mythos.

In his analysis of underground movements, entitled *Subculture* (1979), Dick Hebdige notes that the avant-garde subversions of art and culture, which included *International Times* and *New Worlds*, was developing a particular focus: 'By the early seventies, these tendencies had begun to cohere into a fully-fledged nihilistic aesthetic and the emergence of this aesthetic together with its characteristic focal concerns (polymorphous, often wilfully perverse sexuality, obsessive individualism, fragmented sense of self, etc) generated a good deal of controversy amongst those interested in rock culture.' The style and content of the Jerry Cornelius novels fit precisely into this template and counterculture.

In his book, *Bomb Culture* (1968), author, jazz musician and underground poet Jeff Nuttall offers a description of 'cool' which exactly describes Jerry Cornelius. 'The cool element prefers the casual fuck... [and] exchanges passion for movement... the cool element is the element that responds to James Bond; the cool element wears dark glasses, is faceless.'

The whole world invaded by Jerry, his family, friends and foes is one drenched in the pop culture of rock, drugs, promiscuity and wild parties. The emphasis is on being 'kinky'. It is the language of the sixties and seventies, and people are judged by their sexuality and outward appearance. In the background is a constant soundtrack of jazz, blues and rock music. Jerry listens to Zoot Money, the Beatles, Jimi Hendrix, Hawkwind, and is lead guitarist of the Deep Fix, the name of Moorcock's own band.

It is here that reality and fantasy merge. Hawkwind's 1985 album *The Chronicle of the Black Sword* was based on the Elric cycle, and included the song 'Needle Gun' about Jerry Cornelius' weapon:

> *Feel my pin prick tattoo your spine*
> *Give it a minute, your life's entwined with mine...*
> *It's gonna make you run*
> *Needle gun...*

Hawkwind epitomise the psychedelic movement, celebrating as they do the use of hallucinatory drugs and space age fantasy. Song titles include, 'The Psychedelic Warlords (Disappear In Smoke)' (1974), 'Reefer Madness' (1976) and 'Levitation' (1980). One song written by Moorcock and recorded by Hawkwind is the rock'n'roll stomping 'Kings Of Speed' which mentions characters from the Jerry Cornelius books:

> *Between you and me Mr.C.*
> *I think we have what these boys need...*
> *You're gonna get a tasty trip*
> *On Frank and Beesley's rocket ship.*

Michel Foucault comments on the important role rock music plays, claiming it is 'a cultural initiator: to like rock... is also a way of life, a manner of reacting; it is a whole set of tastes and attitudes.'

To appreciate the Jerry Cornelius books the reader should be well versed in popular culture — particularly rock culture. The Jerry Cornelius books, like many of Moorcock's novels, are postmodern texts which, like many rock songs, satirise culture and express chaos and fragmentation in an increasingly pluralistic world through pastiche, collage and parody. Moorcock attacks the metanarratives of religion, politics, war and morality and replaces them with pop culture and eclectic art forms.

Jerry Cornelius acts like a rock idol, and as a messiah he is 'sacrificed' when he goes out of fashion. George Melly in *Revolt Into Style* (1970) noticed how decadence and rebellion become accepted into mainstream culture when revolt becomes a style or a fashion, and this seems to be the fate or demise of Jerry. He begins life as a hip rebel — suave, deadly and sexy — but by the end of the sequence (*Condition of Muzak*) he is unfashionable and mocked: 'The best performers had either died, decayed or fractured, leaving behind them a vocabulary of musical ideas, lyrical techniques, and subject matter, styles and body languages.'

The Jerry Cornelius books remain misunderstood, perhaps because they cannot be easily categorised generically and Melly notices a similar problem for the culture from which the books are generated. He realised that pop is an ersatz culture that 'could be said to offer a comic strip which compresses and caricatures the social and economic forces at work within our society. It draws no conclusions. It makes no comments. It proposes no solutions.'

The Cornelius books use surreal devices such as collage, juxtaposition, dreams, internal logic. Interestingly, Hebdige describes the dynamic of a subculture in which 'The chaos coheres as a meaningful whole' and these novels perhaps make more sense as an overall sequence than as individual novels.

The tetralogy is carefully structured in four parts with its exposition, development, recapitulation and coda. The three unities of time, place and action are fractured, as is the mimetic notion of character development. The plot for each novel is non-linear and characters frequently change role or personality. Each novel is episodic and more concerned with mood, shape and colour, like music or an expressionist painting. Moorcock describes the structure of the second novel, *A Cure For Cancer*, in the following way: 'It starts with the diagnosis of the problem; here is a society in decay... The chapters get shorter, the rhythm gets more staccato.' Like a tune, the plot has different shapes, climaxing in the middle and then fading, after a sequence of riffs and melodies. The underlying motif is one of entropy and its effect on plot and character. Tragically, there is no cure.

The reader begins to doubt the reality of Jerry's adventures, which are sometimes expressed in language evoking a drug trip. In chapter five of *The Final Programme* Jerry's adventure has been straightforward until reality begins to warp unexpectedly: 'Jerry, now unaware of who or where he was, felt himself being dragged from the sea. Someone slapped his face. What, he wondered, was the nature of reality after all?' The reader wonders if the action in the previous chapters really occurred or if Jerry has been hallucinating and fantasising at a 'fun fair'. This is the first of many alienation devices used in the Cornelius novels, which disturb the narrative and create a nightmarish quality. Time disintegrates, as does text, character and setting, because all are subject to the laws of entropy.

The Final Programme begins like a detective narrative with its mystery, chases and MacGuffins, but it suddenly, and seemingly randomly, shifts in emphasis and atmosphere, becoming a mythological study of the twentieth century — with its inventions and the cynicism caused by moral decay. When it was first published critic Judith Merril called the book 'evil', which surprised Moorcock who had written it as satire and irony. His aim had been to produce a narrative with 'a character who accepted the moral questions without discussing them', and for this reason, the book was considered daring or even shocking. Moorcock wanted his audience to be active and questioning. As he explained in 1976: 'Part of my original intention with the Jerry Cornelius stories was to "liberate" the narrative; to leave it open to the reader's interpretation as much as possible — to involve the reader in such a way as to bring his own imagination into play.'

The four original Jerry Cornelius novels create an illusion of surrealism and randomness, but each has a carefully devised overall scheme using internal referencing and the use of regular motifs and repetitions. Like traditional fantasy and science fiction, the world of the novel has its own internal logic. Moorcock writes, 'All this... should give the effect, among others, of time in a state of flux, men in a state of introverted confusion, close to fugue, and so on. But its internal logic is straight forward... To "explain" all this, to editorialise, would be to break the mood, break the dramatic tensions, and ruin the effect I was trying to achieve. The apparent obscurity should not confuse the reader because the narrative should be moving so rapidly that he shouldn't care if he doesn't understand every reference.'

Moorcock is using a popular and unorthodox style to challenge his readers, using episodic narrative, alienation devices and, like Bertolt Brecht, another artificer, by making the human being the object of enquiry.

The first Jerry Cornelius novel, *The Final Programme*, is a conscious rewrite of two early Elric stories called 'The Dreaming City' and 'While the Gods Laugh' (both 1961). Moorcock himself explains: 'In late 1964, I was casting around for a means of dealing with what I regarded as the hot subject matter of my own time — stuff associated with scientific advance, social change, the mythology of the mid-twentieth century. Since Elric was a "myth"

51

character I decided to try to write [Jerry Cornelius'] first stories in twentieth century terms.'

This translation works effectively and the parallel is explicit. A direct comparison of both openings reveals a group waiting for each Eternal Champion. A band of mercenary warriors wait for Elric to lead them to raze his old kingdom-city of Imrryr, while some scientists await Jerry Cornelius to lead them to his father's postmodern chateau to find a secret microfilm.

The descriptions of the two incarnations of the Eternal Champion present clear similarities. Elric is the albino wizard-Emperor whose 'bizarre dress was tasteless and gaudy and did not match his sensitive face and long-fingered, almost delicate hands'. In comparison, Jerry Cornelius is graceful and mysterious: 'He was very tall and the pale face framed by the hair, resembled the young Swinburne's.' The choice of Swinburne is interesting as he, like Moorcock, is an artificer and a dandy; and there is no doubt that Elric and Jerry are shadows of the author.

Instead of being a magician like Elric, who can conjure elementals, Jerry is an ex-Jesuit who has lost his faith. Drugs have replaced magic in terms of altering perception and casting fantastical spells upon the mind. Music and sex have also replaced magic and superstition as ways of transforming the self, and for overcoming entropy.

Other comparisons are clear: Yrkoon the evil sorcerer has become Jerry's brother Frank; Cymoril, Elric's only love, is now Catherine, the sister with whom Jerry has an incestuous relationship; even Elric's faithful old retainer Tanglebones has been anagrammatized into John Gnatbeelson, the butler. Elric fights with his chaos sword, which sucks the souls and life force from its victims, giving strength and energy to its wielder. Similarly, Jerry kills opponents with his unique and mysterious needle gun, a powerful hypodermic full of deadly narcotics, and we discover that he strangely feeds off others in a vampiric sense never fully explained. 'He found that he didn't need to eat much because he could live off other people's energy just as well.'

A study of the language shows the change in style from romance to postmodern parody. Elric's confrontation with his adversary has him using archaic magic to open a door, 'I command thee — open!', which for Jerry has become the sardonic challenge, 'Throw in your needle and come in with your veins clear.' Next, the albino prince summons Arioch, Duke of Chaos, to protect him, but Jerry makes do with a 'nerve gas grenade' that has much the same effect. Gods and demons have been replaced by weapons, such as LSD gas or conventional guns. Jerry becomes the self-styled Messiah of the Machine Age.

The crowds in the city have become faceless and anonymous, like the many-headed creatures described in fantasy novels which in *The Final Programme* are 'snake-like' or 'a tired pyramid of flesh'. Similarly, the whole of Europe becomes 'a boiling sea of chaos' made of 'fragments of dreams and memories', reminiscent of landscapes confronted by Elric or Corum. Chaos and random flux create a maelstrom of disorder as time begins to run out in a world that cries out for a messiah. Elric flies off on the back of a mighty dragon: Jerry poses in a Duesenberg limousine, dressed like a pimp.

Jerry is an icon of pop culture: a comic book secret agent as well as a 'cool' rock musician. But he is a reluctant messiah who seeks only the solace of a womb-like enclave where he is protected from each catastrophe. He rejects his status as popular hero for the preferred life of drugs and decadence. He lives in a very real London of the 1960s where the myth of happiness is dominant: 'London was alive with flowers... their scent hung like vapour in the beautiful air. And people were wearing such pretty clothes, listening to such jolly music; the first ecstatic flush of a culture about to swoon, at last, into magnificent decadence, an orgy of mutual understanding, kindness, tolerance.' Jerry becomes a symbol of this disposable age. He is a victim of fashion, dressed in the costume to suit his role or mood, and his identity is signified by his changing fashions and attire, paralleling the fickle pop stars who regularly change their image with each passing trend.

Jerry is also an assassin in an age of famous assassins, such as Lee Harvey Oswald, James Earl Ray and Charles Manson. Jerry dresses like a 'dude', listens to pop music and jazz and, as the incarnation of the Eternal Champion in the modern era, represents chaos with his liberated and ambiguous sexuality and his youthful rebelliousness. 'It was a world ruled by the gun, the guitar and the needle, sexier than sex, where the good right hand had become the male's primary sex organ.'

The Final Programme questions identity and sexuality through the motif of the hermaphrodite. Moorcock seems to be interested in exploring gender roles and questioning cultural models and assumptions. An enduring image of the sixties is that of the androgyne or transsexual, most explicit in pop icons such as David Bowie and his chameleonic characters. Commentary on sexual ambiguity and changing ethics is particularly emphasised. For example, Jerry conjectures about seventies London and predicts that 'the true aristocracy who would rule the seventies were out in force: the queers and the lesbians and the bisexuals, already half-aware of their great destiny which would be realised when the central ambivalence of sex would be totally recognised and the terms male and female would become all but meaningless.'

In the later novel, *The City In The Autumn Stars* (1986), Manfred and Libussa are to be merged into a similar hermaphrodite, an alchemical and mystical experiment re-enacting the classical myth of the melding of Hermaphroditos and Salmacis. That particular experiment fails, but the plan to create a messiah in *The Final*

Programme succeeds: 'He had breasts and two sets of genitals, and it seemed very real and very natural that this should be so.' The intended irony is made explicit when the hermaphrodite emerges from the computerised womb and its first words are the absurd greeting, 'Hi, fans!' Rather than being god-like, the hermaphrodite becomes a parody of the androgynous figure of 'camp' pop.

The novel ends with bathos as the 'messiah' drowns all its followers and considers this to be 'A very tasty world'. It is a comment on society's need for messiahs and heroes, and presents the dangers and futility of hero-worship or the self-destructive element inherent in much fundamental religion. The cults of Scientology, EST, Divine Light and the Moonies all found success in the UK of the sixties and seventies.

The film of *The Final Programme*, directed by Robert Fuest and released in 1973, was originally meant to star Mick Jagger, but instead the lead role went to Jon Finch. In the final scene, instead of the hermaphrodite, the emerging creature is a Neanderthal, presumably representing the regression of mankind's evolution. Moorcock disassociated himself from the film, which now seems far too camp to do the novel much justice.

The second Jerry Cornelius novel, *A Cure for Cancer* (1971), is darker than the first, with its lengthy descriptions of war-torn cities leaving societies and individuals the victims of anomie. Moorcock is interested in exploring how people and institutions confront the loss of order, and Jerry becomes a character exhibiting the same symptoms as Colin Wilson's 'Outsider', who is frustrated, paranoid and obsessed with sex. Wilson explains that 'The Outsider is a man who has awakened to chaos' and similarly, Jerry is one who has transcended the constraints of morality and of physics, being free to time travel at will and resurrect himself. Although free, he questions and seeks his identity, playing a multitude of roles. His stories read like nightmares or bad trips, full of guilt and neurosis. While Wilson's alienated anti-hero may end up a visionary or a saint, Jerry achieves only ephemeral messianic status, or a parody of it.

As the Eternal Champion, he is resurrected within the multiverse and has become a negative image of himself, with ebony black skin, black teeth and long, white hair. Jerry is still an individual with psychedelic tastes, wearing a panda fur coat and a turban with peacock feathers. Nobody questions his odd appearance or his dramatic change, and his own family accept his eccentricities. He has become a symbolic figure.

A dandy assassin inhabiting a science fiction landscape, he now owns a 'shifting' machine that unlocks the megaflow of the multiverse, allowing its operator to travel through the time streams. When activated it exposes 'all layers of existence at once' and seems to need rock music to energise it. The shifter creates webs that lead to all the alternative existences that are being played out concurrently. This is the 'megaflow' described as moonbeam roads, which weave a web between the alternate worlds. Jerry's black box diffuses and randomises, transporting individuals into another time or plane, where a similar life, with differences, can be acted out. This brings new hope and possibilities.

Jerry remains an agent of chaos, bringing anarchy with his sabotage and battles against conventionality. The word 'astatic' is used by Moorcock to describe the flux and disorder. His opponents represent order and institution, particularly the grotesque Bishop Beesley who slows down time and rides his 'utopia machine' in an attempt to relocate 'the virtues of the past'. For Beesley, law and order can only come about through suffering. Likewise, Jerry's brother Frank suggests 'We must limit imagination' in order to regain organisation and stability — reminding us how our society can stifle creativity.

In *A Cure For Cancer*, Moorcock parodies 'order' in his portrayal of the US army, who have become Nazi-like dictators, while a character called Himmler is merely a seedy nightclub owner. General Cumberland's speech about the marines leading Europe into war with their 'American strength, American Manhood... American bullets... American virility' is a painfully satirical comment on the Vietnam War, a reality in the background when the novel was written. Moorcock distances himself and the reader from the true horror through his use of comedy, but makes a direct political point, as Moorcock himself explains; 'I was substituting England for Vietnam to bring the war home; to say the same awful distortion of ideals could occur here and we could be its victims.' Moorcock parodies a particular and stereotypical American attitude; a militant xenophobia against communism, homosexuality and liberalism, all of which are cancers that must be 'cured'. Moorcock is commenting on modern imperialism and the chapter headings illuminate this point, including a paragraph from Hitler and an advert for a toy Polaris submarine. For Moorcock, order is the domain of the military, the Church and science, while chaos finds its energy in music, parties and drugs.

Eventually, London is destroyed with napalm and chemical warfare until in the final quarter of the novel Jerry remembers his only reason for continuing: 'There's some hope... There's a chance of love.' And he looks once more upon Catherine's body in the morgue, and manages to temporarily reanimate her with his own body heat. In the coda we are presented with Jerry and his sister, whose lovemaking melts the snow in a romantic finale, before she dies once more. Love is the only thing left for Jerry, and the only activity or diversion which interests him.

Jerry's reality is disturbingly mutable, but his is the world we all experience, one of passions, chaos, fear, 'bad trips' and guilt. The dissipating world in *A Cure For Cancer* echoes the frustrations and emotions in our own minds. The war-torn world is beyond

Jerry's power to save, so he turns to individualism and the saving of Catherine. For every person the world is only what inhabits the individual mind.

The third Jerry Cornelius novel, *The English Assassin*, is subtitled 'A Romance of Entropy', and gives a detailed, if non-chronological account of the slow demise of an alternative Edwardian Britain where a technological utopia has fragmented into a dystopian pantomime. Within the novel itself, various alternatives are offered, often regressing into decay and destruction, or celebrating a fin-de-siécle decadence. Moorcock dismantles the logical sequence of the narrative, so that it becomes episodic and multiplicitous. Here lies the essence of his 'multiverse': being able to see many possibilities at once. Moorcock has stated: 'I'm not confused by multiplicity — I'm delighted by it.' Plurality and ambivalence is a strength not a weakness. Just as Moorcock is fascinated by how the same characters react in different situations, so is he obsessed by the concept of a multiverse of alternatives, tracing how a particular society confronts an alternative history. In *The English Assassin,* Britain is gripped in the 1900-75 war where the air is filled with zeppelin airships while music-hall singers entertain at the end of every pier. This was the beginning of the literary trend known as steampunk, a style more fully developed by Moorcock in *The Nomad Of The Time Streams.*

While the first two Cornelius books are dynamic and splintered, the last two books have a slower pace, representing the slow heat death of the universe. Moorcock quotes Rudolf Clausius' famous discovery in 1865 that 'the entropy of the universe tends to a maximum', and the Jerry Cornelius novels are an attempt to describe this dissemination with his fragmented prose in an attempt to uncover 'the nature of the catastrophe'. The new themes were best served by a new metaphor borrowed from thermodynamics and psychology: the concept of entropy. For the

New Worlds writers it became a metaphor for the breaking down of conventions and structures. Science writer James Gleick, in his popular book *Chaos*, defines entropy as 'the inexorable tendency of the universe, and any isolated system in it, to slide towards a state of increasing disorder.' Entropic fiction tends to emphasise alternate states of mind, while subverting the conventions of character, plot, time and space.

For Moorcock, entropy equally applies to people, places and time. Entropy represents the inevitability of death and decay, but many of his novels, particularly the Cornelius mythos, explore how humans overcome death and attempt to create the best quality of life from what they have. When Jerry finds a wingless butterfly, Bishop Beesley, representing order, wants to destroy it, but Jerry, standing for chaos, identifies with it and saves it. The wingless butterfly is a perfect image for the enigmatic Jerry Cornelius. Moorcock has written, 'life should be enjoyed to the full and its responsibilities taken seriously.' Jerry escapes death by continually reincarnating within the multiverse.

Jerry Cornelius is strangely absent in this third book, suffering from catatonia and hydrophilia, he has spent a year or more in a box under the sea. He is found as a smelly bundle washed up on the seashore, still alive and conscious, screeching and looking like 'a mad gull'. The book is content to follow more closely the other characters of the melodrama as they ship Jerry's body to Dubrovnik. His body becomes the grail this time, initiating the adventure. It was with this episode that Moorcock believes he correctly predicted the horrors of the Dubrovnik corpse boats in the Balkan civil war.

In a short interlude interrupting the narrative of *The English Assassin*, the following words are attributed to Prinz Lobkowitz: 'It would be pleasant, I think, if we could somehow produce a completely blank generation — a generation which has not acquired the habits of the previous generation and will pass no habits on to the next.' The concept of 'the blank generation' was one that was later introduced into protest music by the prototype punk singer-songwriter Richard Hell, who influenced Malcolm McLaren. Music critic Jon Savage recalls, 'The Blank Generation laid out the attractions of vacancy: not just being or looking bored, but the deeper vacancy of the subconscious.' This notion stems from the idealism that each individual has the right to unlearn all that they have been socialised into. While there may be some good to be learned from history and culture we do not want to repeat the horrors of the Holocaust or Vietnam, and Moorcock writing in the sixties and seventies represented the utopian movement of anarchism.

Britain itself in *The English Assassin* is a victim of chaos, falling into entropy, disintegrating and slowly melting in the intense heat. The character who stands for order is the bumbling Major Nye, with his old school tie, English country garden and his inability to show affection or emotion. He represents the old-fashioned and paternalistic traditions of Empire, Oxbridge and the armed forces, and his death near the end seems to signify Britain's crumbling heritage.

Jerry himself is the most ambiguous character, concurrently a sentient corpse in a box, 'a rotting creature which had lain amongst the debris and sheep-dung in the gloomy interior of a tower', or the skeleton of a twelve-year-old boy. Uncertain memories abound, with Jerry as a guerrilla storming Wordsworth's cottage and as a child watching his grotesque mother have sex with a stranger, 'grunting in unison as orgasms shook their combined thirty-eight stones of flesh'. The most mysterious moments occur when the Cornelius family and friends are enjoying Sunday roast and it seems that Jerry is not present, but there is an unnamed boy who falls asleep and is ignored like the ghost of a dead child. Only Catherine refers to him and knows that he is having a nightmare. The reader is left to presume that this is Jerry himself, appearing like a phantom, the illegitimate child whose fantasies, nightmares, trips, time travelling adventures of espionage and messiahship fill the pages we are reading.

The English Assassin is a gloomy book filled with horror. One of the most disturbing passages describes Una being gang-raped and the reader is left with no doubt that this world is collapsing physically and morally. The only response Jerry can give is to ignore the catastrophe by contentedly singing to his ukulele before snoozing on the deck of his boat. The final image of the novel is the bombing and destruction of the seaside resort as Catherine waves, 'Goodbye England.' Jerry, it seems, is not really interested in world affairs and the possibility of global destruction and neither is he particularly concerned with his own messianic status. He only wants a peaceful quiet life away from power struggles and to be alone with Catherine. Jerry, and perhaps Moorcock, has given up hope for England and now the only chance for salvation is to be found in good old-fashioned love.

When asked to define entropy, Moorcock explained: 'We use up a lot of energy, collapse and grow cold… I believe in a sense that human love conquers entropy and that you'll find running through a lot of my books.' This is romantic idealism: love and passion are the only remedies for restoring the human spirit.

The Condition of Muzak presents Jerry's finest performance, and indeed, the novel won the 1977 Guardian Fiction Prize. We are led through another series of episodic personal mythologies, including Arthurian allusions, the underworld of Notting Dale, world politics and show business encapsulated under the all-encompassing metaphor of the harlequinade. Jerry, once again, is many things and many people: an anarchist, a lover, a king, and mainly, 'the bravest dandy of them all'.

During one fancy dress party Jerry is 'feeling the loneliness most painful when one is among friends' when he complains to a passer-by, 'I used to believe I was Captain of my own Fate. Instead, I'm just a character in a bloody pantomime.' The characters begin to take on the identities of stock-types from Commedia dell'Arté or the harlequinade: a theatrical tradition that places the same characters in different scenarios. Typical themes involve unrequited love, mistaken identity and cuckolding. Jerry is always hoping to be Harlequin who is quick witted and wily with a huge sexual appetite. This aptly describes one aspect of Jerry but the suggestion that he is only an adolescent dreaming up masturbatory fantasies is implied more strongly. He is, in fact, only Pierrot, the frustrated dolt. John Rudlin's notes on Pierrot in his handbook *Commedia dell'Arté* could be a character study on Jerry Cornelius: 'Gives vent to feelings only when alone... A loner, an observer of the follies of others, but unhesitatingly faithful to... Columbina for whom he suffers eternally unrequited love. Childlike... At times, however, the best he can scheme for is to escape the punishment others have in store for him.'

It turns out that Una is the real Harlequin and is Catherine's chosen lover. Catherine is Columbine, the rational and self-sufficient woman who is the object of most people's desire. Jerry's sister Catherine remains an enigmatic character in the novels, later becoming the main character in her own novel along with Una Persson. Catherine becomes Jerry's only purpose or hope; she provides a genuine love for him to respond to. She is always the catalyst who provokes and sustains the action. Their interdependency is highlighted near the end of the novel when her reflection in a pool shows his face rather than hers.

The unsavoury Bishop Beesley, an agent of law who constantly pursues Jerry, is an amalgam of Pantalone and Captain Fracasse, aggressive and authoritarian. Frank is Scaramouch, the stirrer. All the city folk are playing their roles in the scenario, improvising, acting out set-pieces, rehearsing and performing behind their social masks. This leads to one of the most colourful set-pieces in *The Condition of Muzak*, which describes Christmas and lists an extensive dramatis personae from myth and pantomime. Characters in the novel become the stock-types from Mummers plays, mystery cycles, pantomime, fairy tales and mythology. Miss Brunner, the school ma'am, becomes Britannia, a prototype Mrs Thatcher; Major Nye, the imperialist, is Saint George; Mrs Cornelius is Widow Twanky.

In fact, Mrs Cornelius is one of Moorcock's most bizarre and enduring creations. She appears in other novels, most notably the Col Pyat novels, himself a character in the Cornelius books. Mrs C is a foul-mouthed, libidinous grotesque straight from Dickens or Peake. Jerry appears to be very dependent upon his mother, with whom he has an Oedipal relationship. She drinks gin, belches and uses expletives unthinkingly, and yet she is always attractive to men. Her reactions are ludicrous and show her to be indomitable. For example, during a picnic with her family, her lover is shot before her eyes, but she turns to Frank and comments, 'Still, yer've got ter larf, incha?' She is most cynical about Jerry, who is in stasis in his vampiric box. She does not understand his achievements or his aims, and yet she is incredibly perceptive, and the reader understands her attitude when she states, 'Iber-bleedin'-natin' 'e corls it! Master-fuckin'-batin' I corl it!'

This evaluation of Jerry could well be accurate, and the ambiguity of his character allows this to be a distinct possibility. Perhaps Jerry is no more the messiah of the age of science, as much as he is some grubby adolescent wanker. Moorcock has intimated as much. In a private letter answering this very question he replied: 'Jerry is everything. Everyone.'

Like anthropologist James George Frazer's account of Saturnalia, with its sacrificial mock king or Lord of Misrule, so Jerry Cornelius is the sacrifice, the scapegoat for his generation, the clown who is mocked, criticised, blamed and punished as an example. Miss Brunner sneers at Jerry; 'He wasn't his world's Messiah... He was his world's Fool.' But this adds up to the same thing. He is a messiah, in the same way as Dostoevsky's idiot is, except that Jerry will always return to play Pierrot once again.

Moorcock has created a literature that forms a critique of mainstream culture and the accepted forms of institutional convention. He uses folk or popular culture to satirise authority, much as Rabelais did in the sixteenth century. Jerry Cornelius becomes the everyman who experiences all our hopes, dreams, failures and pain.

5: OSWALD BASTABLE
'I'M NEITHER A NIHILIST NOR A MILITANT.
I HAVE NO PARTY.'

The Oswald Bastable trilogy is also known as The Nomad of the Time Streams. Oswald Bastable is a child hero in E Nesbit's *The Treasure Seekers*, who Moorcock imagines grown up. These tales are early examples of steampunk and alternate world fiction. John Clute, in the *Encyclopedia of Fantasy*, describes Moorcock as 'a central twentieth century exponent of urban fantasy, and of both gaslight romance and steampunk, and he can take primary responsibility for the temporal adventuress.' These comments relate mostly to the Bastable books and the character Una Persson, who also appears in the Cornelius and End of Time sequences.

The first novel, *The Warlord of the Air*, was first published in 1971; then the trilogy was reprinted a number of times and collected in omnibus form, before being rewritten and expanded for the 1993 Millennium edition, *A Nomad of the Time Streams*. Initially I shall refer to the original editions, then later on highlight the changes and additions made to that later publication.

Eric Rabkin, in *The Fantastic in Literature*, argues that *The Warlord of the Air* is a pure fantasy text by his definition. He claims that true fantasy should change the perspective and 'ground rules' of reality for both the reader and antagonist, such as in Lewis Carroll's Alice books. Oswald Bastable unwittingly becomes a 'chrononaut', travelling forwards and backwards into alternative yet recognisable eras within the twentieth century where parallel characters live out 'realities' which echo our own political history.

The novel is clearly inspired by HG Wells' *The War in the Air,* and the tone of the narrative is that of H Rider Haggard or Jules Verne. Just like Haggard's *She* and Edgar Rice Burroughs' *A Princess of*

Mars, *The Warlord of the Air* begins with Moorcock claiming to be the editor of a manuscript written by another. Here he claims his own grandfather met Oswald Bastable and wrote down the tales leaving the reader with a challenge: 'It is up to you to decide if what follows is fiction or not.'

The first encounter with Oswald Bastable is in 1902 as a filthy stowaway and opium addict, claiming to have flown giant airships and fought wars in an alternative Britain of the future. His time travelling comes about as a result of an earthquake in a holy city in the Himalayas. When he is rescued by Major Howell of the Royal Indian Air Police, Bastable quickly realises he has travelled over seventy years into the future to 1973. This version of 1973 sees the British Empire still thriving. Churchill enjoys dominion as Viceroy of India and Mick Jagger has a walk-on part as a helpful lieutenant. The world is split into empires: the American colonies include Vietnam (the war still raging when the book was first published). Howell explains to the newcomer how Pax Britannica has brought peace and 'a stability to the world it has never known before'.

It appears that poverty has been banished from London under King Edward VIII, and for Bastable this neo-Victorian future seems a utopia, with the only possible threat coming from 'Nihilists, Anarchists and Socialists'. His politics are typically reactionary (or simplistically naïve), but over the course of the three novels he begins to understand more about human nature and how political power corrupts all forms of idealism.

The technology that Bastable now experiences first hand becomes central to the narrative and the style of these early steampunk texts. References to computers, kinematographs and marconiphones abound, but most iconic are the descriptions of airships, flying machines and weaponry, which are extensions of early inventions from Victorian industrialisation. Most impressive are the giant zeppelin-like airships and dirigibles — sometimes over 1,000 feet long and able to carry 400 passengers in a triple-decked gondola. Bastable finds work on a passenger airship, but the story finds greater impetus when he joins the crew of Captain Korzienowski (the real name of writer, steamboat captain and one of Moorcock's great inspirations, Joseph Conrad).

It is while working on board *The Rover* that Bastable realises to his horror that one of his passengers is the infamous terrorist Count Rudolfo Guevara (namechecking the greatest revolutionary hero of the twentieth century). It is Guevara's convincing arguments that force Bastable to reconsider his own political perspectives: the Count demonstrates the inequalities of the Empire where 'The Indian starves so that the Briton may feast' and that destroying souls rather than bodies is 'evil of the worst kind'.

Guevara's consort is the ubiquitous Una Persson — the enigmatic temporal adventuress with the uncanny knack of popping up at the right time like some deus ex machina. She returns in all three novels, using trickery and charm to get herself into positions of strength, depending on each situation.

The eponymous warlord appears late in this book in the guise of Chinese pirate-of-the-air General OT Shaw (Shuo Ho Ti), who, in the tradition of a Bond villain, hopes to take over the world. China offers a different threat under his vision: 'The future lies here, in China... Europe is dying.' His method involves 'Project NFB': a nuclear fission bomb.

The ending explores the morality of nuclear war and the stockpiling of arms, with Bastable left contemplating 'the enormity of what had happened'. The guilt and feeling of responsibility stays with him for the next two novels, shaping his change in attitude and personality.

The Land Leviathan (1974) is subtitled 'A New Scientific Romance', which links it closely again with the popular fiction of

HG Wells. Moorcock purports to have found a manuscript written by Bastable in his own late grandfather's hidden safe. In this new version of reality Una Persson is a bandit chieftain who describes Bastable's condition as being 'trapped forever in the shifting tides of Time'. He will become one of the League of Temporal Adventurers, along with Una, Jerry Cornelius, Karl Glogauer, Lord Jagged et al.

This time Oswald Bastable finds himself in 1904 where the world is in the chaotic grip of various wars and barbaric madness; where Europe and Britain have been 'reduced to ash and rubble'. One stark episode occurs in the wasteland which once was East Grinstead in West Sussex. Una Persson has been captured by a tribe of savages, 'hung spread-eagled' on a trellis, but rescued at the last minute by Bastable and escaping in a mechanical tunnelling contraption.

War machines terrorise whole nations, in the shape of U-boats, cannons, airships and 'self-propelled armoured carriages called land ironclads'. Even biological weapons are mentioned, such as 'the Devil's Mushroom, Brighton Blight and Prussian Emma, which causes haemorrhaging from all orifices.' A British sergeant admits bleakly that 'it could go on until the last human being crawls away from the body of the chap he's just bashed to bits with a stone.' The tone is bleak and pessimistic.

The most feared individual is the Black Attila, an African-American leading a jihad against the whites. His real name, General Cicero Hood, conflates two sympathetic figures: a humanist Roman philosopher and a celebrated English folk hero. His desire is to create a New Ashanti Empire, beginning with an attack on the United States with the singular intention 'to liberate the black peoples'. Himself the son of a slave, Hood exclaims how: 'It is time the black man had a chance to run the world. I think if he can rid himself of the sickness of European logic, he can make a lasting Utopia.' From this point *The Land Leviathan* becomes an examination of the changing and abhorrent attitudes about racial difference.

Bastable has a number of experiences that change his general outlook. When he flies to South Africa — known here as Bantustan — he meets President Gandhi, who has created a haven of civilisation and pacifism, which becomes a kind of Tanelorn against which all other nations are to be compared. Back in the USA, Hoover and Joe Kennedy are linked with white supremacy and the Ku Klux Klan also makes an appearance. It is when Bastable witnesses the dignity and courage of the black workers being beaten by hysterical cowards in white hoods that he begins to shift his political bias. The moral of the story is eloquently expressed by Bastable in the following way: 'There could be no such thing as a "righteous" war, for war was by its very nature an act of injustice against the individual, but there could be such a thing as an "unrighteous" war — an evil war, a war begun by men who were utterly corrupt both morally and intellectually.'

Michael Moorcock admits to being unhappy with *The Steel Tsar* (1981), the next book in the series, on first publication, thus feeling compelled to alter and expand it for the Millennium omnibus (discussed in more detail below). This novel examines the philosophy of anarchism with a brief mention of the writings of Kropotkin. Moorcock seems keen to point out that anarchism is much maligned and misunderstood. The public image is one of nefarious bombings and terrorism, whereas anarchism is actually about individual liberty from authoritarian rule. Particular reference though is made to Nestor Makhno, who appears as a character in his own right. Makhno was a communist guerrilla leader and commander of the Black Army in the Russian Civil War. Moorcock has often expressed his support of Makhno: in the introduction of *The Great Rock'n'Roll Swindle* (1981), written around the same time, he states: 'For me, Nestor Makhno is the spirit of romantic, active anarchism,' and he dedicates that book to his memory. Makhno's ideals (sometimes labelled Makhnoism) are closely allied with platformism, which emphasises the Kropotkinesque philosophies of mutual aid, self-sufficiency and collective responsibility. Makhno fought for the decentralisation of power, seeking to abolish capitalism and the state by creating assemblies and communes which ran under self-regulation and practised free exchange with other communities. Moorcock clarifies his views in his 1993 introduction: 'Paternalism and centralism, the bane of capitalist as well as socialist politics, are for me the permanent enemy of democracy.'

The focus of the novel, however, is in fact Stalin, who appears as Josef Vissarionovich Djugashvili (Stalin's real name). Stalin was also known as the 'Man of Steel'. Historically, Stalin, as the first General Secretary of the Communist Party in the Soviet Union, became an autocrat whose reign of terror oversaw millions killed in purges via his secret police and in the gulag labour camps. He also famously made a pact with Hitler. In this version of Earth in 1941, Djugashvili is the leader of the Nationalist rebels in Russia. Japan and Russia are at war; the British Empire is still extensive if benign; the Ottoman Empire includes much of Africa and the Middle East and is now an Islamic force to be reckoned with. The Japanese Empire attacks British targets, believing Britain began the war with its bombing of Hiroshima. In alternate world fiction we see history repeating itself, as if fate demands it on every plane of existence, or perhaps because human nature is so predictable that the variations are slight. Bastable has finally worked out one truth: 'The greater our ingenuity at inventing weapons, the worse the wars become.'

Oswald Bastable experiences a moment of self realisation when he reflects: 'I have been fated... to witness the worst examples of insane warfare (and all warfare, it seems to me now, is that) and having to listen to the most ridiculous explanations as to its necessity from otherwise perfectly rational people.' But the most important lesson is: 'No individual is responsible for War — we are all, at the same time, individually responsible for the ills of the human condition.' This neatly sums up the philosophy of collective responsibility.

Makhno understands, like Mahatma Gandhi, that fighting only gives 'further excuse for brutality'. He dares to decry Djugashvili as an 'authoritarian hypocrite'. Mrs Persson too espouses the same sense of anarchism when she suggests: 'At root we are victims of the comforting lies we tell ourselves, of our willingness to have leaders, religions, of our wish to shift responsibility onto others, whether it be politicians, Gods or creatures from other planets.'

Another important character is Cornelius Dempsey, whose heroic actions make him a martyr figure in the League of Temporal Adventurers. Interestingly, Moorcock dedicated the Millennium edition to Michael Dempsey, the name of one of his early publishers and a close friend. (As an aside, the earlier Granada edition is dedicated 'To my creditors, who remain a permanent source of inspiration.')

Moorcock believes his rewrites for the Bastable trilogy have improved the narrative and the biggest changes occur at the end of *The Steel Tsar*. In general summary, most of the changes are to names, thus emphasising the inter-connectedness of the Eternal Champion cycle. Some of these appear forced or unnecessary. The new sections either stress the anarchistic philosophies of mutual aid and the avoidance of armed conflict, or further outline Moorcock's literary and metaphysical theories of time and space. Below I shall outline the notable changes made for the 1993 Millennium edition.

In *The Warlord of the Air*, Captain Harding of the Loch Etive airship becomes Quelch to link with the Second Ether series, and humorously the irritating American passenger expressing racist views evolves neatly from Egan to Reagan. One change which suits Moorcock's purpose but loses both political potency and symbolic meaning, is the alteration of Guevara to Count von Bek.

For *The Land Leviathan* Moorcock adds a name to one of the best short sequences of the novel, which occurs in England. The previously unnamed and barbaric King of East Grinstead, with his 'bestial grin', who would not be out of place amongst the hordes of Granbreton in the Hawkmoon books, is now named Major John — a reference to the unremarkable Conservative Prime Minister of the time, John Major.

The final two chapters of *The Steel Tsar* contain extensive rewrites and whole new sections that allow the author to meditate upon his themes. Von Bek's appearances add very little and even then he rather strangely transmutes into Zenith the Albino, which makes his inclusion appear somewhat forced. Many of the new discussions add explicit exposition to the trilogy's implicit themes, especially regarding the cosmic balance and how 'an infinite number of other versions of oneself existed throughout the multiverse'. The most memorable piece of tampering occurs when Professor Marek asks: 'Are we anything other than curious maggots, burrowing through the rotting cheese of History?' On this note, Oswald Bastable makes the decision to join the League of Temporal Adventurers to make amends for his failures as an individual. It seems there is little more we can do.

Moorcock's original intention is summarised in his 1993 preface: 'These three simple stories attempted to explore some of the ideas — especially about imperialism and racialism — which I have explored in different ways in my Jerry Cornelius and Colonel Pyat books. The sequence is also my homage to those not-quite-forgotten writers of pre-1914 Britain.'

6: DANCERS AT THE END OF TIME
'MY CHARACTERS ALWAYS TAKE OVER.'

Embraced within the Eternal Champion cycle is another series of novels, The Dancers At the End of Time. In these, Moorcock employs comedy, fantasy and an elaborate style straight from the literary *fin de siècle* to portray the clash of two cultures. If Jerry is the failed messiah then the other avatar of the Eternal Champion with the same initials, Jherek Carnelian, is the eternal child — naïve and inquisitive.The three novels *An Alien Heat* (1972), *The Hollow Lands* (1974) and *The End of All Songs* (1976) are now anthologised under the title *The Dancers at the End of Time*. There are also three sequels to the trilogy: *Legends From the End of Time* (1976) consisting of three short stories, a novel called *The Transformation of Miss Mavis Ming* (1977 and which is also a sequel to *The Winds of Limbo*, 1965) and the novella *Elric at the End of Time* (1981), which connects the series more closely to Moorcock's Eternal Champion cycle. The protagonist is Jherek Carnelian, a derivation of Jerry Cornelius, thus expanding Moorcock's ever-widening multiverse.

The initial trilogy presents a bizarre, satirical and lyrical vision of an anarchist utopian future in which a repressed puritan, Mrs Amelia Underwood, comes into conflict with a promiscuous aesthete, Jherek Carnelian. Once again we get a glimpse of the eternal struggle between law and chaos, this time with comic consequences and a large cast of grotesque characters involved in witty dialogue and black comedy. The style is tragi-comic, also owing something to nonsense and absurdism. Moorcock believes that 'Comedy — like fantasy — is often at its best when making the greatest possible exaggerations' and these novels contain some of his most extreme and larger than life characters. *The Dancers at*

73

the End of Time is evidence that Moorcock was writing humorous fantasy and science fiction long before either Douglas Adams or Terry Pratchett popularised the forms.

The first novel, *An Alien Heat,* is a comedy of misunderstanding and human error. It begins at the end time of our universe where 'the human race had at last ceased to take itself seriously'. We are presented with an entropic world where decadence and sensuality dominate the mainstream philosophy giving an immediate parallel to the bohemian Decadent movement —nineteenth century subversive writers such as Oscar Wilde, Charles Baudelaire, Arthur Machen and MP Shiel. Moorcock also acknowledges George Meredith and once again the poet AC Swinburne as influences and this is evident in the ornate language and use of irony and metaphor.

Moorcock creates a culture with new psychological dynamics. There is a question as to whether this society is a utopia or dystopia, but it is certainly a presentation of exaggerated anarchism — that is, freedom from authority and laws. On the positive side this is a society with no problems regarding greed or jealousy, because possessions are unimportant. All desires are freely catered for, and each individual has the power to create any physical object from thin air or fulfil any dream using a ring which allows anything from their imagination to come true. The end of time is an amoral culture in which incest and promiscuity are dull, everyday activities. Jherek regularly consummates his physical love for his mother, The Iron Orchid, as if it were perfectly normal; and for him it is. However, time travellers from other eras and worlds are predictably horrified.

At the beginning of *An Alien Heat,* Jherek Carnelian and his mother enjoy a picnic on the beach, eating sumptuous foods while discussing the unfamiliar ideas of 'virtue' and 'self-denial' about which Jherek has read but is uncertain of their meaning.

The reader quickly learns that the inhabitants of the end of time are obsessed with abstract experiences and show disinterest and naivety towards concepts of old age, time and death. They are gods grown bored. They all have the power to resurrect anyone who is unfortunate enough to die; otherwise they are immortal, so death has lost its sting and truth or reality is constantly questioned and ambiguous. Jherek asks his mother rhetorically, '... but what is particularly interesting about the truth?' Life has become a vulgar game. A time traveller comments upon their lifestyle, 'You play mindless games without purpose or meaning', which sums them up quite neatly. Having no aim or purpose in life creates boredom and ennui.

Like a comedy of manners, *An Alien Heat* involves courting, love, jealousy and witty repartee. The style of language is romantic and the plot uses the traditions of farce to sustain and develop plot lines. The narrative revolves around the unlikely relationship between the innocent, idealistic Jherek and the Edwardian puritanical housewife Mrs Amelia Underwood, who is transported millions of years forward in time. Jherek decides to fall in love with her as an amusing experiment and his lovemaking involves insincere games as he fails to appreciate her different socialised assumptions. Jherek plans their future together in his imagination: 'If she fell in love with him tomorrow (which was pretty inevitable, really) there were all sorts of games they could play — separations, suicides, melancholy walks, bitter-sweet partings and so on.' The comic ordering of these activities shows his ignorance of true sacrifice, for suicide is just another silly game if resurrection is possible. However, Mrs Underwood's idea of love is also insincere. She speaks proudly of a steadfast commitment to her distant husband and their 'institute of Christian marriage', which is lawful even if there is no love involved.

Once again the extremes of chaos and law are distinguished

here with a romantic stalemate between a hedonist and an ascetic, two philosophies that Moorcock successfully satirises. Jherek is the bohemian with magical powers and his artistry lacks taste and subtlety, while Mrs Underwood remains virtuous and is sensible to her 'duty' and dignity. She finds him depraved and corrupt, while he is continually confused and frustrated. Mrs Underwood, who has chosen order and stability, sees it as her mission to convert Jherek to her standards. She could be free of her repressed and sheltered upbringing and fulfil all her fantasies and yet she chooses to reject all enjoyment and lead a dull temperate life.

The tone is then set for tragedy until Jherek travels back in time to Edwardian London, following his new-found love. Unfortunately, Jherek there begins to take himself seriously and mourns his loss of irony; 'It is no longer a game!' he cries. In an uncharacteristic moment of self-realisation he recognises that his love is genuine and this is certainly a new experience — one that also involves pain.

Moorcock's London is the grimy underworld of Ben Jonson and Charles Dickens, filled with corrupt stock-types and squalid criminals' dens, such as Jones' kitchen, also known as 'The Devil's Arsehole'. Jherek's evaluation of our world is summed up in his cry of disbelief: 'Many of their pastimes are not pursued from choice at all.' Jherek becomes an allegorical figure caught up in crime, and it is only when he is hanged, wrongly accused of murder, that Mrs Underwood finally declares her love for him. The convention of tragedy is subverted when the reader remembers that, for Jherek, death is no obstacle.

The second book in the series, *The Hollow Lands*, makes good use of farce, particularly the sections involving ridiculous sex-crazed aliens and some Keystone Kop-like policemen, creating a manic slapstick style in the tradition of Victorian pantomime, although the novel is not made up of comedy alone.

The greatest moment of realism occurs when Jherek meets the writer HG Wells, with whom he discusses time travel. Wells recognises Jherek as an eloi, one of the aesthetic race of creatures evolved from humans, as described in his novel, *The Time Machine*. It is significant that Wells appears in these novels as time travel is discussed at some length. Back at the end of time their own scientist, Professor Morphail, has invented a time machine, but he describes the paradox and problem for all time travellers: 'If one goes back to an age where one does not belong, then so many paradoxes are created that the age merely spits out the intruder as a man might spit out a pomegranate pip which has lodged in his throat.'

Jherek manages temporary shifts but cannot control his movement like the nomads of the time streams can.

The residents at the end of time, such as Bishop Castle and Gaff the Horse in Tears, become quickly bored with their lives and create different realities depending upon their whims and moods, fashioning houses, new games to play and even whole worlds — all in intricate detail — by the use of their energy rings.

There is much aesthetic debate in the novel about the difference between reality, realism and the artistic product. The residents' fake realities are more detailed and preferable to actual reality, although they lack the authenticity of smell and texture. However, Jherek begins to crave a more passionate and chaotic form of expression and Robot Nurse laments the loss of romance. In a moment of Moorcockian self-reference, the author has her quoting from his earlier fantasy, *The Knight of the Swords*, which describes a primeval world of magic and mythology filled with 'phantasms, unstable nature, impossible events, insane paradoxes, dreams come true, dreams gone awry, nightmares assuming reality'. Here Moorcock seems to be reminding us of the importance of fantasy, which gives us the ability to dream and escape from reality.

The book ends with a discussion regarding self-denial, with Jherek still failing to grasp such a pointless concept. Jherek's final words — 'what is "self denial"?' — are the final words of the book: he still has much to learn. The reader is reminded that love is a game in which the chase is more fun than the apprehension.

The End of All Songs continues the courtly dance and is the most subtle and graceful of the trilogy, full of baroque language and descriptions of elaborate social conventions and leisurely lifestyles. The cycle is concluded with Jherek learning to be unhappy and experiencing jealousy for the first time. He realises that his world is artificial and rediscovers his own humanity. The novel's structure is unusual, beginning with catharsis, followed by denouement and resolution, and ending with tension and further development.

The conflict is a continuation of the complex relationship between the ordered discipline of Mrs Underwood, who follows the utilitarian ethic that 'If one leads a moral life, a useful life, one is happier', and Jherek's libertarian world of freedom and imagination. Moorcock is emphatic in his preference for the latter and eventually even Mrs Underwood begins to question her own beliefs. The culture of the Edwardian middle class is parodied for its ridiculous constraints upon natural behaviour and for the repressed anguish and pain caused by these suppressions. Jherek and Mrs Underwood begin to understand each other, as she becomes more sensitive and less callous:

'I love you,' he said. 'I am a fool. I am unworthy of you.'
'No, no my dear. I am a slave to my upbringing and I know that upbringing to be narrow, unimaginative, even brutalising... And now I see that I am on the verge of teaching you my own habits — cynicism, hypocrisy, fear of emotional involvement disguised as self-denial.'

Her original intention was to educate these 'noble savages', but she ends up admiring their simple honesty. While chaos implies pleasure, order demands suffering. Mrs Underwood continues to criticise her world, which we recognise as our own. 'You do not know my world, Jherek. It is capable of distorting the noblest intentions, of misinterpreting the finest emotions.' Moorcock's critique of Western culture is explicit and as the new Adam and Eve, Jherek and Mrs Underwood have a romantic chance to start the human race again.

Just as carnival comedy ridicules those who represent status and authority, so these novels are full of witty satire and damning black comedy that laughs at the constricting dominant culture. The anarchic culture at the end of time is offered as a more attractive place, full of magic and innocence. The characters are colourful and shocking, like those pop culture rebels ostracised by the mainstream. There is the morbid Werther de Goethe, who dwells in loneliness and self-pity, living out the archetypal existence of the anguished poet and rejected lover. Mistress Christia, the Everlasting Concubine, represents extreme sexual amorality, willing to try any form of pleasure — however perverted.

As Jherek's true father, Lord Jagged of Canaria acts as the catalyst for the entire narrative, bringing together the two protagonists and manipulating their actions like a puppet master conceiving jests and fabulations. His role is similar to that of the Warrior in Jet and Gold from Moorcock's Hawkmoon books. He is identified as both Mephistopheles and Machiavelli and also takes on the role of judge in the nineteenth century, with the ironically changed name of Jagger, linking him with one of the most subversive pop stars of our own times. These outrageous characters are reminiscent of the hippies. Cosmic irony is evident in Lord Jagged's controlling the characters' destinies, manipulating their futures and performing experiments with his friends and family as test-subjects. This theme of God as the archetypal ironist laughing at our expense is one that recurs in Moorcock's work. In the short story 'Elric At the End of Time', it is strongly implied that Lord Jagged is Arioch, the God of Chaos, who Elric serves.

The Dancers at the End of Time explores the juxtaposition of two cultures. Once again, order has a repressive and stifling effect upon its inhabitants, while chaos gives room for creativity and artistic endeavour with the added danger of passion and pain, which can also be destructive.

The Dancers at the End of Time sequence is a postmodern montage and pastiche of various modes of writing. Moorcock's visionary novels work on many levels, satirising Protestant morality and comparing it to utopian libertarianism, while also experimenting with fantasy and comic forms of literature.

7: GLORIANA
'I DON'T WRITE MUCH POETRY — I LIKE DOING PASTICHES OF POETS, BUT I DON'T RECKON MYSELF A GOOD POET.'

Arguably Moorcock's most literary fantasy, *Gloriana, or The Unfulfill'd Queen,* which won the World Fantasy Award and the John W Campbell Memorial Award in 1978, owes much to Mervyn Peake's Gormenghast trilogy. Scholar Peter Caracciolo described the novel as 'that apotheosis of heroic burlesque' and this is certainly an apt summation. It parodies Edmund Spenser's sixteenth century allegorical poem, *The Faerie Queene,* subverting the romantic literary notions by making a humanist comment on Spenser's moralism. *Gloriana* is not merely a pastiche of Queen Elizabeth I, but is also a dark, psychological exploration of human conflict in which the Queen's palace and castle, with its hidden corridors and rooms, represents the mind, riddled with repressed guilt, hypocrisy and corruption. Its themes of chaos versus law, sexuality and its use of depth psychology can be seen as a consummation of the literary experiment that Michael Moorcock began as editor of *New Worlds.*

Gloriana was first published in 1978 and then revised in 1993 in response to feminist criticism from Moorcock's friend Andrea Dworkin, who argued that the climactic, penultimate chapter, as it was originally written, could be seen as a justification for rape. This perturbed Moorcock, a feminist sympathiser, so whereas Queen Gloriana had originally been the victim, her role was switched to that of violator.

Before this questionable denouement, in which Gloriana finally controls the antagonist of the novel, Quire, sexually, she learns of her own shocking conception: she was raped by her own father, presenting the brutalism of some men who seek sexual power within relationships. This is the worst side of chaos. Moorcock has written articles from a feminist standpoint arguing that 'women are constantly and systematically silenced by men, by male-dominated society.' In *Gloriana* fulfilment is found when the woman rediscovers her rightful power and the man learns to know fear.

The revision omits two pages (pp375-6 of the 1978 Fontana edition) and adds five new pages (pp362-6 of the 1993 Orion edition). In the original, Quire rapes his Queen and then illogically switches personality as if schizophrenic: 'Quire jumped back, careless of his own unfinished pleasure, and his face was suddenly quite innocent.' However, in the revised edition Gloriana threatens Quire with a knife between his legs and discovers her own true identity while taming Quire, her evil alter ego: 'She was no longer Albion. No longer justice, mercy and wisdom, no longer the personification of righteousness, the hope and ideal of her people. She was Glory. She was self... He stumbled back... The beast cowered for an instant in his eyes before fleeing entirely exorcised, and leaving him looking at her with the awe some ancient hermit might have lavished upon the face of a deity.' This gives a better justification for Quire's reversal and strengthens Gloriana's character adding weight to the consummation of chaos and order, and significance to the romantic ending where Quire becomes Arthur in an ideal kingdom of knights and chivalry. The romantic and classical traditions finally unite. Moorcock uses the metaphor of balance to embody Renaissance notions of harmony, furthering his motif of the duality of chaos and order.

Gloriana is not an individual but a symbol personifying the state of Albion, with 'personal decisions subservient to the needs of the state.' She is seen to hold the state in equilibrium, with all laws and values personified in this one god-like figure. She is deified, and yet the reader soon discovers her to be a flawed and sympathetic figure, eternally sexually dissatisfied (as the novel's subtitle suggests). 'Her Majesty's Curse' refers to the fact that she cannot achieve orgasm, or any satisfactory release from her responsibilities. Even orgies and other decadent experiences remain hollow and unfulfilling for her. This lack of fulfilment brings her continued torment. Gloriana is neither virtuous nor a virgin; she regularly practices sexual deviance and masochism within her seraglio and has many bastard children, yet she remains unfulfilled.

Gloriana's femininity is essential to the plot and purpose, and is an important part of Moorcock's own philosophy. Whereas traditional masculinity celebrates violence and danger, Gloriana rejects such male obsessions: 'But I fear war and all that attends it... Violence simplifies and distorts the Truth and brings the Brute to eminence.' The traditional 'feminine' qualities are the strengths required to lead a liberal society.

Gloriana is a woman in a world where all other leaders are men and even her own state is run by men. She has learned to play her part but remains only a symbol and not an individual. 'She was like a splendid flagship... cheered on by everyone who watched her glide across the water, and none to know that, below the waterline, she had no rudder and no anchor.' Her constant dilemma remains her balancing her monarchy with her humanity. Gloriana loses her individual identity for the sake of her nation, Albion, as her priority lies with her subjects and kingdom — her own satisfaction and well being coming second. Although Gloriana is the main character, Moorcock uses the technique of omniscient author, allowing the reader insight into the minds and perspectives of other characters.

Captain Quire represents chaos. He is an amoral libertine who murders, deceives or corrupts all he meets before cheating his way into Gloriana's affections. His name adds a hint of irony, linking him with religion and church, and the narrative use of 'chorus'. The author describes him as 'a demon', a malevolent spirit that manipulates and brainwashes people, such as minor characters Alys Finch and Phil Starling, who he tames as pets. He easily seduces Gloriana, for it is the monarch's raging lust for sexual gratification that allows chaos to disturb the order of Albion. The Platonic ideal of love and unity is corrupted by the selfish pursuit of desire and pleasure.

Gloriana's Lord Chancellor, Lord Montfallcon, provides the balance between order and chaos. While Gloriana is the symbolic figurehead, the state's ship is truly steered by this devious politician. Montfallcon is obsessed with maintaining order and tradition and is dedicated in his love for the queen, whom, we finally discover, is his own granddaughter. Even he admits that peace is a charade; only he knows and plots behind the façade of order, hiding all true corruption and conspiring with criminals in order to maintain the myth of glory and the golden age. Ironically, it is his servant Quire who shatters the veneer of harmony. Shamed, Montfallcon recedes into self-immolation and his relapse is part of Albion's downfall. Montfallcon plays a similar role to Lord Jagged and the Knight in Jet and Gold who control the balance through manipulation and artifice.

It is quickly apparent that Albion as a utopia is counterfeit; it is really inhabited by whores and blackguards, and the members of the Privy Council are mere fops. The myth of peace and justice is sustained by regular masques and festivals, which romanticise the reign of Gloriana and help the public to believe in the myth of perfect harmony. Montfallcon is an idealist who wants order by hiding chaos, which, in essence, means the so-called utopia of Gloriana is little different to the tyranny of Hern, her own father. During one episode of unsolved murder, Sir Tancred, one of the Queen's knights, is accused without having motive or the temperament. Montfallcon is ruthless in his speculation, seeking to retain order at all costs: 'He hoped that Tancred were not innocent. It was better to have a culprit, cut and dried, than a court that simmered in speculation. Rumour, gossip, suspicion and fear. He could sense them now, threatening his Golden Age, his Reign of Piety, his Age of Virtue.'

Moorcock explains that the palace 'represents not only the brain, the conscious and unconscious minds, but behaviour and motivation too'. The dark inner passages and secret rooms behind the walls are a metaphor for Gloriana's mind, which has fallen victim to entropy; walls are crumbling, while members of the court are bored, entertaining themselves with traditional pursuits and masques. It is almost to relieve the torpor that the Queen accepts the unpopular Quire as her lover, but he brings crime, lust and selfishness into the peaceful 'utopia'. Moorcock suggests that the chaos brought by Quire was necessary for a court full of hypocrisy and deception. It is only Quire who brings the Queen and her courtiers to life with his own energy, finally making them look at themselves and their own lives with some honesty. In this sense, Quire is an essential part of each one of us.

Although *Gloriana* is not an historical romance its links with history are clear. Elizabeth I was born a bastard of King Henry VIII and Anne Boleyn, and some historians intimate that Elizabeth was the issue of a rape and possibly violated as a child by the infamous Thomas Seymour. Historians commonly note that her main priority in all her decisions and actions was 'the weal of the kingdom' and while her famed virginity is questionable, the fact that that she was a strong female leader is undoubted.

Quire seems to be an allegorical amalgamation of two historical characters who disturbed life in Elizabeth's court, namely the Earls of Essex and Leicester; both rogues. The Earl of Essex was unruly and flirtatious, initiating internal conflicts and threatening national peace, while Lord Robert Dudley became the Earl of Leicester and, it was assumed, continued a love affair with the Queen. Sir William Cecil, Elizabeth's Principal Secretary, upon whom Montfallcon is loosely based, was suspicious of Dudley, thus losing favour at court.

As well as the extensive royal household of over 1,500 people, Queen Elizabeth also had other favourites who visited her rooms, including the infamous alchemist John Dee, who would cast her horoscope. Doctor Dee was a sixteenth century mathematical philosopher who dabbled in theatrical illusions and magical practices such as astrology — in those days regarded as a science. In *Gloriana*, Dee, whose name remains unchanged, is secretly and painfully in love with his Queen, comically lusting after her as he talks politely. 'He bowed again, sucked in a breath or two. (Blood of Zeus! These pantaloons will make a eunuch of me yet!)' Dee also becomes the mouthpiece explaining Moorcock's beloved multiverse with its intersecting spheres and parallel worlds.

Structurally the novel is based on four theatrical pageants. During the Twelfth Night Festival, Gloriana is presented as Freyja, a facet of the ancient European goddess, Frigg, who was considered a goddess of sexuality and an aspect of the Mother Earth. The poem written by Wheldrake invokes the Norse gods of Asgard, and knights re-enact the battle of Fire and Ice, another dualism, before Ragnarok, the last battle, from whose ashes is born the new world and Albion. Ragnarok, also known as the Twilight of the Gods, is both a beginning and an end. It symbolises the birth of a utopia, but also signals the end of order and the coming of chaos. In *Gloriana*, Quire is the equivalent of Loki, the mischievous god who brings disorder.

During the Mayday Spring festival, things start to go wrong, but not until we are treated to Wheldrake's Spenserian pastiche called 'Atargatis; or the celestial virgin', adding a new character to Moorcock's complex mythology. Gloriana is the May Queen, another incarnation of Mother Earth also connected with fertility rituals.

The Accession Day Tilt is the chance for a summer tourney with its affirmation of chivalry, where Quire, as Palmerin, the eponymous hero of an ancient European epic poem, becomes the Queen's new champion. As the court falls further into decadence and entropy, autumn brings the annual Feast of Bacchus, an orgy to delight all the senses, particularly the sexual and visual. The sexual games become more explicit and less tasteful, while Gloriana struggles to play her expected roles as mother, protector and, most difficult, goddess. Until her moment of individuation, she is an automaton manipulated firstly by Montfallcon and then by Quire. Indeed the entire court is led a courtly dance by Quire until all the members of the privy council and the Queen herself are no better than toy maker Master Tolcharde's clockwork harlequinade. As Dr. Dee remarks: 'And who can say... whether these creatures are any less alive than we, of flesh and blood?' Here Moorcock reminds us of the recurring symbolism of the Commedia dell'Arté in his work, a motif that represents the cyclical lives, deaths and myths that invade the multiverse.

Even though *Gloriana* is a single volume, it cannot escape the boundaries of Moorcock's immeasurable multiverse, and a certain number of familiar names appear within the castle walls. Jephraim Tallow is a minor figure skulking in the shadows, and interestingly, is the protagonist of Moorcock's first novel, *The Golden Barge*, which evinces a similarly baroque style and psychological themes. The poet Ernest Wheldrake reappeared in the 1991 Elric novel, *The Revenge of the Rose*, which is also the most 'literary' of his sword and sorcery novels, in which Wheldrake became Elric's companion on the quest for his father's soul, composing sonnets and odes on heroic and philosophical themes. In *The Dancers at the End of Time* Mrs Underwood quotes a poet called Wheldrake from Edwardian England, whose verses read like those of Swinburne, and Moorcock has explained that 'Swinburne attacked himself as Wheldrake'. A third recurring character in *Gloriana* is Una, who, while also a character in *The Faerie Queene*, is undoubtedly related to the immutable temporal adventuress Una Persson from the Jerry Cornelius and Oswald Bastable series. She certainly represents the most sensible and human side of the female.

Life in the court is tortuously dull, so the characters spend their energy and time amusing and diverting themselves with theatrical entertainments, sexual exploits and political intrigue, until they gradually dissipate, receding into brooding despair. The novel lays down some positive and challenging ideas; not least that life is a precarious balance between virtue and vice, and that it is only when these opposites are reconciled that we begin to experience the completeness of our own existence. The sexual union of Gloriana and Quire provides an allegory for the fulfilment of the male and female complement, which has found expression elsewhere in Moorcock's work in the symbol of the hermaphrodite. Life is a sensory experience where desire must be fulfilled and feelings expressed, but only in a society where there is some acknowledgement of responsibility and medium of control.

Moorcock, in claiming his own purpose in writing the novel, states something similar: 'I was trying, if this doesn't sound too nuts, to reverse the idealising allegory of *The Faerie Queene* and give Gloriana back her humanity. I'm also very fond of Quire. I would say that love, in the form I most admired it, was respect for, and celebration of, the individuality of others.'

In Moorcock's novel, the state represents authority, while Quire becomes a symbol for the id — particularly the complex desires of the Queen herself. The climax of the revised novel is literally an orgasm, fulfilling the ultimate aim of the carnival, which is the birth of a new world, and Quire's coronation is the triumphant crowning of the carnival king. romanticism and classicism finally unite but the ending is just another masque. The final sentence is an echo of the opening, thus completing the cycle of the seasons.

In *Gloriana* the reader is presented with a liberal authority that is paternalistic on the outside but corrupt within — a model familiar to Western politics today with the advent of media-manipulating spin-doctors and constant allegations of 'sleaze'. The novel invokes symbolic images of power on both an individual and national scale.

8: COL. PYAT
'IT LOOKS AS IF COL. PYAT MIGHT MAKE A BRIEF
APPEARANCE AT THE YOUNG VIC ON DECEMBER 6TH.'

The four volumes, which compose the memoirs of Maxim Arturovitch Pyatnitski (Colonel Pyat), are referred to as the Between the Wars sequence. *Byzantium Endures* (1981) presents us with Pyat's precocious adolescence and pretentious engineering ambitions as he grows up in Odessa and St Petersburg. The Russian Civil War disrupts his plans and he finds himself unwillingly fighting alongside Makhno, the anarchist revolutionary folk-hero who also appeared in *The Steel Tsar* (1981). In *The Laughter of Carthage* (1984), Pyat gets caught up in the proto-fascist political machinations of 1920s Turkey and Italy before becoming a travelling speaker for the Ku Klux Klan in the United States. *Jerusalem Commands* (1992) evokes the glamour of Hollywood; Pyat stars in silent movies, but during filming in Egypt he is tricked and brutally abused to the point of breakdown, after which he returns to his ideals of creating a technocratic utopia. The final volume, *The Vengeance of Rome,* examines Pyat's involvement with two of the most frightening tyrants of recent history, Hitler and Mussolini. Pyat had already indicated his sympathy for Mussolini's vision in *Jerusalem Commands*: 'Adolf Hitler, representing proud masculinity, and Benito Mussolini, representing the spiritual, feminine side of the fascist discipline. Left alone, I think they would have made perfection.' He is a character and narrator with whom it is difficult to empathise.

One particular experience motivated Moorcock to explore these twentieth century horrors: 'I increasingly identified with my Jewish family... Then, on a ship coming into New York harbour one day, I was again shocked by the blatant antisemitic remarks from the German and Russian passengers from which I fled without protest. That cowardice led me to conceive and write, in the course of the past twenty-five years, a sequence of novels in which I hope to explain how the Nazi Holocaust drew strength from many such acts as mine. My work became a form of atonement in which I took on the burden of guilt.'

These are the most consciously political of Moorcock's novels, exploring the uses and misuses of power in the twentieth century. In his system, order is a synonym for tyranny and authoritarian control, while chaos symbolises the more liberal theories of individual autonomy and community, best represented by anarchism, which rejects authority and hierarchy. Moorcock believes that any form of authority, left or right wing, ends up oppressive: 'Uncertain of the consequences of genuine social change, nervous of the "Chaos" manifested through the incoherent euphoria and destructiveness of the mob, leaders of revolutions fall back on the methods of their predecessors in an effort to restore the rule of "Law."'

The Pyat tetralogy has one distinct voice; the first person narrative of Maxim Pyatnitski, which expresses the opposite views to those held by the author. By his own admission Moorcock had difficulty sustaining the writing, particularly the final novel, *The Vengeance of Rome*, professing that the material was 'hard, dangerous stuff to contemplate'. Moorcock clearly rejects the evils of tyranny, and campaigns against prejudice and sexism, but here takes on the demanding task of entering the consciousness of a bigot. His disclaimer is made immediately in the introduction to *Byzantium Endures*, where Moorcock claims he has only edited the manuscript of 'a liar, a charlatan, a drug addict'. This technique of claiming editorship of someone else's work is a device for creating a greater sense of realism — Moorcock has used this technique to good effect in previous novels, particularly the Bastable novels which follow similar themes. Moorcock wants the reader to believe that Pyat is a real person involved in actual historical events, so when Moorcock appeared in an interview in London in 1993 he arranged for an actor playing Pyat to interrupt him from the floor and to take over his 'own' story. Pyat is a character, or at least a name from the Jerry Cornelius books, and is loosely based on a real person from Moorcock's neighbourhood in Notting Hill, London.

On reading the memoirs, it becomes clear that while the young Pyat dreams of scientific progress with his utopian vision of a technocracy, as an older man he has become excessively reactionary and mentally unbalanced. It is the older, schizophrenic Pyat who writes in retrospect, and he interrupts his own stream of consciousness with his vitriolic asides 'uttered' in a sometimes impenetrable mixture of English, Russian and Polish, giving the impression that he is shouting directly at the reader. While much of the prose is clearly structured — following his unorthodox journeys chronologically — the text is continually disjointed by his wilder and darker passions, and it is in these moments that the reader encounters the real man and confronts his most violent thoughts.

Moorcock uses the distasteful, if sometimes amusing, voice of Pyat to create a distancing for the reader, explaining: 'With each sentence there is the possibility that it is not the truth. So each sentence has to contain or contribute to an ambiguity.' The reader is left to make moral choices based on the memoirs of an unreliable narrator.

The novels are a biased history of the terrifying political changes in the twentieth century, particularly those leading into the Russian Civil War and then the Second World War. Pyat, whose racism and invective are forced upon the reader, is an unsympathetic character and an egotist, whose anti-Semitism led to the book being heavily censored in the USA. Pyat also has the ability to continually reinvent himself, and like the Eternal Champion he can be 'resurrected' with a different identity depending on the context. He is more despicable than the usual picaresque rogue, being guilty of murder, torture, rape and intolerant racism, although the ultimate irony is that he is probably himself a Jew — a Jewish anti-Semite.

Pyat's beliefs are firmly rooted in the ideal of Plato's Republic, with its specific components and strict order, symbolised more specifically by the Byzantine Empire which in his view brought order to the world with its utopian vision of law, authority and nationalism. One problem with Plato's 'utopia' is that there was no room for poetry and creativity, hence no fantasy, amidst its militant sexism. Pyat's obsessive fear is that Islam and Judaism will bring chaos upon the Western world and this xenophobia is aimed at the cities of Carthage and Jerusalem and what they represent mythologically and politically.

The four cities in the titles are significant. Byzantium (now Istanbul) became a powerful force under the control of Alexander the Great and in the second century BC its army supported Rome in its various wars, becoming, in effect, the Eastern wing of the Roman Empire. Eventually, in 330AD, Constantine the Great rebuilt the city as a new imperial capital, renaming it Constantinople, and it remained one of the richest cities in Christendom. After the schism of 1054, the Orthodox Church achieved independence from the Pope and developed its own sacraments, doctrine and rituals, with which Pyat closely identifies however insincere his faith might be.

Carthage in North Africa probably began trading as early as the ninth century BC. The dominant religion involved human sacrifice to gods such as Baal, and was therefore considered by Christians to be pagan, or even satanic. In ancient history Carthage forged a respectable empire led by the likes of Hannibal, but was eventually defeated by the more powerful Roman Empire after which it became a centre of Christianity. The city continued to change hands and in the sixth century it became part of the Byzantine Empire until it was seized by Arabs.

Jerusalem became the focus of the Crusades, in which European Christians fought Muslims for control of the Holy Land. Still tormented by political conflict, Jerusalem is a holy site for Christians, Jews and Muslims, and though Palestine was the birth land of Christ, it is interesting that the most important Christian power resides in Rome.

The so-called 'Eternal City', Rome was the capital of the greatest empire in ancient Europe. After Julius Caesar's death Augustus brought the republic to an end and appointed himself the first Emperor, forging a force of law and order on a world scale. Rome contains the Vatican state, home of the Roman Catholic Church, which boasts more than a billion followers, and as a city it emphatically symbolises power and order.

Moorcock is keen to bring the reader's attention to the death of empires, and by evoking these historically important cities manages to provide a metaphor for the ebb and flow of invasion, and the changing patterns of dominance between different cultures, religions and belief-systems. Byzantium is the Greek city of order and high art, Carthage is the domain of the pagan Oriental, Jerusalem is the home of the Jew, and Rome is the archetype of a fallen, decadent city that once ruled the world. Most of all, these picaresque novels are about a fluctuating period in European history, a time that caused confusion, change, violence and loss; appropriate subjects for fantasy.

In *Byzantium Endures* we are confronted with Pyat's narration and let into the secrets of his strange childhood and upbringing. As an ambitious and pretentious adolescent, Pyat is guilty of arrogance, for if we are to believe even some of his claims, then he is certainly unusually gifted and somewhat unlucky not to have gained fame and public recognition. But the reader is always made to feel suspicious and wary of his arrogance as he tends to promote himself with extreme egomania: 'I felt somewhat godlike... a messiah.' This self-indulgent ranting leads to one of the first of his lengthy tirades in which he rewrites history and mythology, working himself into a frenzy. Because he cannot reconcile his anti-Semitism with his slightly deluded Christian faith he has had to recreate Jesus as a Greek, a prophet in the mould of Plato. 'What can save the world? Not the Jewish-Moslem God... Only the Son can save us. Christ is a Greek'.

He stands firm in the belief that the spirit of the Roman Empire will continue in Russia as long as the nation does not lose faith in the great traditions and the ancient wisdom. Pyat depends upon the authority of such institutional traditions; he needs them to make sense of his own life and to retain a personal identity. The two world wars caused so much change and confusion that the individuals caught up in the chaos depended upon structures and rules to give their lives shape. In Moorcock's multiverse this Eternal Champion is an agent of law fighting against liberalism, although it is ironic that his adolescence is a series of adventures involving illicit sex, smuggling, cocaine and masturbation. Pyat is also a victim of self-deception and the reader begins to lose faith in his perspective.

For Pyat, love is linked to tragedy. His childhood sweetheart Esme is in love with him, but he is too ignorant and full of his own self-importance to appreciate her love. While he sleeps with prostitutes and lives a debauched life, she waits patiently for him. Years later he comes to realise he has feelings for her but she has left to help in the war effort as a nurse. Determined to find her he finally stumbles upon her as a pitiful and dirty prostitute, who tells him indifferently, 'I've been raped so often I've got calluses on my cunt.' This horrific memory continues to haunt him through all four books, becoming a leitmotif for the entropy of romance and sexuality.

Esme personifies Russia in terms of innocence removed — a noble country wrecked by a civil conflict of sectarian warfare — and continuing with this metaphor, Pyat then performs his greatest illusion so far. Being fickle, he is filled with hatred for Esme, accusing her of betrayal and shame for his home, so with a sleight of hand he reinvents both. He renames Kiev the 'Rome of Russia', and then disappears to Constantinople/Byzantium which quickly becomes his true spiritual home ('Tsargrad'), just as later Hollywood becomes his new 'birthplace'.

Esme's reinvention is his greatest act of self-deception. By the second novel, *The Laughter of Carthage*, he resolves to forget that the real Esme exists and with a Frankensteinian bravura creates a new Esme who will not betray him. The new 'Esme' is in fact a thirteen-year-old Romanian whore (and to a Western reader little more than paedophilia). Unaware of his hypocrisy he even admits to himself, 'Oh, Esme my sister... I never wanted you to be a woman.' As soon as he can he sails to the USA and lies to his new Esme, promising to send for her but instead satisfying his lust in brothels, extending his hypocrisy to the extreme: 'I remained loyal in spirit to Esme... (It was at a bawdyhouse, however, I had my first experience of a full-blooded negress).' This is charged with extra irony, as he makes no secret of his vociferous racism. So, still taking cocaine and acting the libertine, Pyat believes in his own innocence and importance.

The USA brings new optimism and a new identity, that of 'Max Peters', but even his faith in the Ku Klux Klan cannot provide the blueprint for the new Byzantium and inevitably he is betrayed by them and once again finds himself rejected. Before the second novel ends, the Holocaust is anticipated before the final testimony of Pyat, allowing Moorcock to compare the techniques of the Ku Klux Klan, who 'staple testicles to a tree', with those of Auschwitz Nazis who 'passed their leisure skinning youths alive'. Not allowing despondency to set in, Pyat, now Max Peters, idealises Los Angeles before he has got there, because, after all, 'The holy wood is where Parsifal discovered the Grail.' It is difficult not to admire his optimism.

Jerusalem Commands is stark in its portrayal of evil, with Pyat becoming a more obvious victim. The most incredible thing about his story is that he survives so many horrors. Pyat in this sense represents us all, the everyman, as survivor of this century and witness to some of the worst atrocities ever committed. This third volume compels the reader to become less judgmental of Pyat, whose message has become sobering and challenging. His most noble comment is delivered amidst a successful time for him and perhaps the moral of the whole sequence: 'Now I have learned that Chaos is God's creation and it is our duty merely to order our part of the universe. Perhaps we are all too slow to accept responsibility. I cannot blame the British Empire, nor the American, nor Hitler, nor Mussolini, without accepting some blame myself.' This jolts the reader from any comfortable distance or moral high ground for there is no place left from which to deflect our self-responsibility.

The memoirs move towards the Nazi concentration camps and the mood grows stark and the atmosphere stifling. Pyat's visions become apocalyptic and demonic after he agrees to commit a real rape for a movie they are filming in Egypt, and the memories become mingled in a haze of hallucinations in which he seems to enter the Egyptian underworld. These nightmares become, in turn, confused with the Nazi vision for 'Order, Security, Strength' and we are shown a glimpse into the horrors of the concentration camps. Pyat, still arrogant, mistakes himself for Osiris who has been buried alive by Set, the lord of darkness, also known as Satan. During his death-like experience he is sexually abused and humiliated by a demoniac hermaphrodite.

Now the aggressor becomes the victim. This time the hermaphrodite is not a symbol of fulfilment, but rather of grotesque brutality at its most repulsive. This episode is written as a montage of dream, memory and myth and it is only when resurrected by Anubis that he escapes the horrors of this century. Moorcock warns us that we need beliefs and ideals to help us to make sense of the chaos; we need visions and ambitions to continue into the future, and we carry within us the spirit of ancestors and generations past.

Pyat is clearly not an anarchist, but Moorcock is, and by presenting reality from a distasteful perspective he makes a strong case against the rise of political authority and tyrannical forms of control. Moorcock stated his views on power in a letter to the *London Review of Books:* 'I'd guess that roughly the same proportions of sadists and psychopaths, useful for genocidal work, exists in any society and emerges at appropriate times. It's apparently impossible for an ordinary middle-class person to imagine the deep lust for power at any price, the violent sexualised fantasies and ambitions of that frustrated sadist who could very easily be a neighbour, a colleague or even a spouse. Most of us would prefer to think such people exceptional. Or fictional. Or foreign. I believe they represent a fairly large percentage of the world's population.'

In *The Vengeance of Rome*, Pyat's exploits become melodramatic and even less believable, as he becomes a confidante of Mussolini and then, once in Munich, intimate with Ernst Röhm and forced into depraved sexual acts with Hitler himself. He witnesses some of the most horrific events of the twentieth century first-hand when finally being consigned to Dachau concentration camp. However, Maxim Pyatnitski is the ultimate survivor. We know from the first book that he has survived long enough to tell his narrative to an author called Michael Moorcock.

After experiencing 'Tangier's notorious shadow world' he sails to Majorca and begins planning his future as Mussolini's partner: 'Inevitably I would add to Il Duce's greatness as he would to mine.' In Pyat's eyes, Mussolini 'brought a dash of romance and tough common sense to politics'. He becomes excited by the right-wing political risings which can only bring order to a chaotic Europe.

Once in Rome he describes the city as 'a huge Hollywood stage' like the sets from films such as *Intolerance* and *Ben-Hur*. He is seduced into an affair with Mussolini's own mistress before befriending the leader's wife. Much to his own surprise Pyat finds himself quickly promoted to the rank of Minister of Overseas Development in Mussolini's Inner Cabinet, selected as a secret emissary to spy on certain members of the Nazi Party in Munich and Berlin.

Pyat quickly gets seduced by Ernst Röhm, the founder of the SA, or 'the father of the Storm Troopers'. Röhm develops a 'profound passion' for Pyat which becomes both possessive and obsessive, even conferring upon Pyat the rank of 'honorary captain in the Foreign Intelligence wing of the SA'.

Through jealousy and blackmail, Pyat finds himself on a dangerous, and frankly ludicrous, mission: to dress as Hitler's recently murdered niece-lover, Geli Raubal, and allow the Führer himself to perform any lewd act he so desires. The passages detailing these acts are almost unreadable, as depraved as anything in the works of de Sade. What makes it more absurdly sinister is how Hitler is referred to intimately as 'Alf'. Pyat tries to reconcile his views by commenting that 'Everyone close to the Führer understood he was an inspirational symbol rather than a practical leader'. It is certainly true that the myth became much greater than the man himself.

What balances our view of the most terrifying figure in twentieth century history is the candid opinion of the delightful Mrs Cornelius: 'They were all such 'orrible ordinary little turds, really. That 'Itler was the worst. Bore the tits off a bull, 'e would.' She remains the most sympathetic character in the novels, always representing the views of the 'common-folk', like a comic Greek chorus.

Through Pyat's narrative voice, Moorcock offers us a reductionist summary of European political history in the early 1930s: 'That the Reds had betrayed the Blacks was almost inevitable, so now we even had Blacks, as well as disaffected Reds and Greens pretending to be White. Enough, Mrs Cornelius remarked, to turn anyone Blue. Meanwhile Hitler's Browns made strategic alliances with men offering the bright multicoloured banners of monarchy.' This colourful overview brilliantly expresses the nonsensical nature of the catastrophe.

As if things couldn't get worse, Pyat is arrested, herded into a truck and confined in Stadelheim Prison where he sinks into self-pity, before witnessing the Night of the Long Knives and the killing of Röhm. Release and further betrayal lead him right into Gestapo headquarters and further confinement. But it is his inventiveness that gives him hope and with a Munchhausen-esque bravura he devises a dramatic escape while testing his one-man airship. He ends up in Barcelona just in time for the end of the Spanish Civil War.

The conclusion of the series is stultifyingly realistic, and full of further denial and self-delusions. By the end, Pyat has become his own myth; the narrative has transcended the individual character and as always Mrs Cornelius makes the most sensible response to this hypocritical lunatic when she says, 'I sometimes wonder if you're real.' Of course he isn't; but tragically the horrors Pyat has narrated are.

The 'Between the Wars' sequence attempts to portray the various struggles for power on both global and individual platforms and Moorcock interrogates such uprisings in history, seeking to highlight and understand forms of cruelty and horror. In Pyat's commentary the reader is allowed an insight into an individual's struggle for internal sanity. It is in these 'historical' novels that Moorcock brings the fantasy of his earlier sword and sorcery novels up to date, for just like the fantasy novels, we see a world in constant conflict — the struggle for power while cities and races rise and fall as a symbol of the flux in human social order.

His extensive research has led him to conclude: 'The Nazi Holocaust had been permitted not just by cynical government decisions in London, Moscow, Paris and Washington, but by thousands, perhaps millions, of minor refusals to confront intolerance and to permit, even promote, prevailing prejudices.' So Moorcock is determined for us to learn from these terrifying truths: 'By reproducing what is familiar to us, rather than taking intellectual and political risks, by dismissing liberal humanism or, if you like, traditional spiritual values, as an unrealistic basis for our actions, we could well create the conditions for another Holocaust even more terrible than the last.'

To his own chagrin, Moorcock has become the 'go-to' celebrity for anything to do with the Holocaust or Second World War. He has spent a great deal of time thinking through the most horrific acts of the twentieth century, and has become very forthright and philosophical. Moorcock has found meanings and continues to challenge us all — not just in fiction but in his thought-provoking and carefully considered non-fiction. We need to heed his warnings.

9: VON BEK
'CHAOS IS AN ATTITUDE NOT A QUALITY.'

The von Bek family have become important in Moorcock's later writing, allowing him to connect books and series by the use of names that constantly reappear, once again allowing him to play tricks with characters, settings and situations. Much of his recent output follows various members of the von Bek family. In 1992, Moorcock anthologized the two von Bek novels, *The War Hound and the World's Pain* and *The City in the Autumn Stars*, as the first volume in the *Millenium Orion Eternal Champion* series. Also added is an early but revised story, 'The Pleasure Garden of Felipe Sagittarius', which is only related because the author changed the name of the narrator from Minos Aquilinas to Minos von Bek. And Moorcock continues to play with names in many of his novels and short stories. For example, the recent short story anthology, *London Bone* (2001), abounds with various von Beks (and its anglicised form, Begg). *Tales From the Texas Woods* (1997) includes a detective story in which the famous Sexton Blake has become Sexton Begg, thus relating even him to the von Bek clan. The link with the Eternal champion is made explicit in *The Dreamthief's Daughter* (2001), presenting Ulrich von Bek as Elric's doppelgänger, and von Bek is also the protagonist of another important novel, *The Brothel In Rosenstrasse* (1982).

However, Ulrich von Bek first appeared in print in 1981 in *The War Hound and the World's Pain,* which was runner up for the World Fantasy Award. This literary fantasy utilises the structures and themes of romantic literature, borrowing its mood and atmosphere from Gothic fiction. It offers a postmodern inversion of one of the main Christian myths (or at least Milton's interpretation as set out in *Paradise Lost*), an apocalyptic vision of the completion of the cycle of creation and redemption in which Lucifer yearns for his own return to Heaven. Here, Satan becomes the most sympathetic character in the book, full of remorse, having grown weary of his struggle to fulfil his duty as enemy of the world. He hopes that his genuine penitence will lead him to his eventual atonement.

He is a tragic figure — a victim of hubris — fatigued by his role as tempter, now a figure of noble pathos. 'He bore an aura about His person, which I had never associated with the Devil: perhaps it was a kind of dignified humility combined with an almost limitless power.' For Moorcock, Lucifer is now more human-like in his frailty, filled with guilt and sorrow, looking through 'melancholy, terrible eyes' and speaking with 'exquisite sadness', telling the protagonist, Ulrich von Bek, how he yearns to be reconciled with God.

Lucifer takes von Bek on a guided tour of Hell, which, unlike Dante's *Inferno*, is a cold and hopeless place, where Satan roams bored but also worried that he may have misunderstood God's original commission. The novel becomes an inversion of the Faustian myth, where von Bek can gain life and rescue his soul from damnation if he can find the Holy Grail, whose restoration will lead to a 'cure for the world's pain'.

Moorcock is not so interested in Christian, moralistic symbolism, but he uses the Grail to portray a romantic notion of love. Von Bek, like Elric for Cymoril, is spurred on by his love for the mysterious and beautiful Sabrina, a servant of Lucifer. Love is a frequent source of energy in Moorcock's work and is the only cure for entropy, the inevitable, slow death of the universe. In Moorcock's work, the Grail can also be a person or a place, and is usually the key to manipulating the time streams of the multiverse.

The reader is forced to revise set assumptions regarding good and evil, now in the guise of law and chaos. The most evil character in the novel is not Lucifer but Klosterheim, ironically a knight of

Christ. Klosterheim symbolises the corruption and bloodlust of the early Church, most apparent in the Holy Inquisition, another Gothic context. Moorcock is presenting the Church as an institution of order and control, and, more controversially, Satan is no longer evil.

Eventually, von Bek stumbles upon the Grail, a simple clay cup, and is told that 'the cure is within every one of us', for each individual is responsible for his own balance and harmony, particularly the balance between reason and sensibility. Von Bek's quest was really to discover freedom from divine powers and fate, and this inevitably leads to cosmic irony. Rather than rely on religion, von Bek's quest is to discover his own identity and he learns that 'one must not seek to become a saint or sinner, God or Devil. One must seek to become human and to love the fact of one's humanity'. The cure for the world's pain lies in self-belief.

The sequel, *The City in the Autumn Stars* (1986), follows the destiny of humanity from an age of superstition to the Age of Reason and the beginning of industrialisation. Claiming to be the picaresque confessions of Manfred von Bek and set in 1794, we meet von Bek on his return from revolutionary Paris. Like his friend, Tom Paine, he had become disillusioned with Robespierre and the Jacobins, eventually denouncing the despotism of the bloodthirsty mob. Bored with politics, von Bek decides to become a hedonist and follow the family motto: 'Do You the Devil's Work.'

Moorcock, it seems, is still unhappy with the final version of the novel after being told by his editor to cut out a third of the original manuscript. The author has admitted that it is 'a book with only a little backbone left'. He has expressed a certain embarrassment about the book's failings, but it is probably better than he imagines. The bombastic language and symbolism are, at times, contrived or ambiguous, but they only add to the novel's poetic and dream-like quality. The overarching themes are those of gender identity and the development of rationality over religion — using the symbolism of alchemy as the transition between magic and science. While the book begins with a strong historical setting, it quickly moves off to the fantasy realm of Mittelmarch via Moorcock's beloved Mirenburg, the perfect city. Stylistically, the novel shifts between comedy of manners and Gothic fantasy.

Von Bek is pursued by two sinister knights, Montsorbier and Klosterheim, who also appeared in *The Warhound and the World's Pain,* and his flight seems pointless until he meets Libussa, the Countess of Crete, who he pursues after falling in love with her. His companion is the ever cheerful Scotsman St Odhran, a student of the Montgolfier brothers and owner of his own hot air balloon, in which they make their frequent escapes. It is when he flies in the balloon that von Bek realizes the potential power provided by these miracles of technology: 'My ascent... by aerial ship was the first moment I truly realized the world had embarked upon a radical new course in which mankind's theories and dreams could now be made reality.' Reason, or law, begins its ascendancy over Romance, or chaos.

In his nightmares, von Bek has vivid hallucinations in which classical mythology becomes confused with alchemical symbolism, always leading him to the image of the hermaphrodite, the ideal fusion of male and female. Visions continue to haunt von Bek to the end. When he finally confronts Libussa he has become so obsessed with his idealized love for her that he allows her to control him and he takes the passive, or traditionally feminine, role in their relationship, symbolized by mercury. Libussa takes the active, male part, symbolized by bronze or sulphur, and these elements are signs of sexual chemistry. It transpires that she is an alchemist waiting for the Astral Concordance that occurs every thousand years, when different worlds intersect, 'to offer harmony, a cure for the world's pain'. This ability to cure all diseases is also the main property of the elusive Philosopher's Stone sought by the alchemists. Her search for balance in the struggle between reason and the supernatural is to be discovered in the conjoining at this time of male and female in the creation of a hermaphrodite. Libussa reassures von Bek that 'the sum of the two of us would be god-like'.

Being a von Bek, he soon finds himself searching for the Holy Grail, meeting on the way the delightful Lord Renyard, the fox king of rogues, who reads Voltaire but suffers from ennui, and the more mysterious Goat Queen. He also witnesses a satanic cult sacrificing a ritual lamb, but learns through a meeting with Lucifer himself that these so-called devil worshippers have nothing to do with him and that even Klosterheim and Montsorbier serve only their own selfish ends. Lucifer gives von Bek the sword of Paracelsus, a sixteenth century alchemist of our own world, who sought the secret elixir, or Philosopher's Stone, that would restore the celestial harmony between the human body and the stars — a cure for the world's pain. His sword was said to contain the devil, which gives a neat parallel with Elric's sword Stormbringer. It was also believed by some that Paracelsus successfully created the artificial man known as the 'homunculus', an obsession later shared by famous English occultist Aleister Crowley, as depicted in Crowley's novel, *Moonchild* (1929). The homunculus is the alchemist's attempt to create a messiah or superman through the use of arcane magic, secret tinctures and occult 'science'.

In *The City in the Autumn Stars*, Libussa is preparing von Bek as her partner in a ritual marriage of sulphur and mercury to create harmony and a new messiah, who will be immortal and omnipotent. This hermaphrodite will be 'a leader who no longer spreads the word of God, but spreads the word of humanity', announcing a new era of science and knowledge. Although the experiment is essentially a failure, von Bek, ironically, learns a great deal about humanity and love. While he has become obsessed with his love for Libussa, her affections for him were seemingly insincere as she only served her own purposes, mainly her search for self-empowerment. Ultimately she is guilty of hubris, believing she can control nature itself. The Grail, symbolic perhaps of love or even God (who remains strangely absent throughout) will not allow the power of the Beast to rule.

The apocalyptic ending is somewhat confusing, but it is the nature of alchemy to be hermetic and obscure: Moorcock brings in arcane symbolism, such as the eagle, which seems to represent Lucifer himself and cannot be controlled by mere humans. Von Bek is also confused and believes, wrongly, that he has betrayed the woman he loves.

Although he loses Libussa, she continues to live in his memory and desire, for he seems to have discovered the true meaning of love. While she was using him for her own end, he quietly confided in her, making the most poignant statement in the book, telling her, 'I love you for who you are. I love you as a human creature.' And so humanity wins and even Lucifer realizes that the world is the realm of men and women now. Fate lies in our hands.

Many of Moorcock's more recent short stories develop similar themes and ideas, most notably in the important story 'The Clapham Antichrist' (originally appearing as 'Lunching with the Antichrist' in 1993). This key story develops the von Bek family history and links Edwin Begg with the Rose, who together have a hermaphroditic child who becomes a messiah leading the world into a new stage in evolution. Similarly, in 'The Cairene Purse' (1990) we learn how Beatrice von Bek falls in love with a hermaphrodite alien and then gives birth to a messiah who dies. These stories are certainly related to *The City in the Autumn Stars.*

Moorcock's original intention was to write a trilogy, as he explained in the forums of Moorcock's Miscellany <multiverse.

org>: 'I originally intended to do three novels — one set in the Age of Religion, as it were, one in the Age of Reason and one in Nazi times — so while the Elric (*The Dreamthief's Daughter*) is the first book in a new series, it's also the last in another!' The third book in the trilogy was abandoned and became the new Elric novel.

Moorcock and his publishers, Earthlight, caused great excitement with the announcement of this new Elric book in 2001 and *The Dreamthief's Daughter* is the first of a new trilogy also linked to the generic name von Bek. Narrated in the first person by Ulric von Bek, an albino living in 1930s Germany, whose life becomes entwined with his doppelgänger — a certain albino demigod called Elric of Melniboné. Before uniting with his alter ego, von Bek dreams of flying on the back of a dragon and tells of his black sword, Ravenbrand. In the first section of the novel the reader gets the German perspective of internal politics and events leading up to the Second World War, explaining how Hitler was seen as a strong leader who would 'bring us stability'. Von Bek, however, quickly sees the error in his nation's judgement and swears to destroy Hitler. He sees that this stability or obsession for order is overly simplistic, and he bemoans the folly of his countrymen who failed to understand that 'human beings are far more complex than simple truth and simple truth is fine for argument and clarification, but it is not an instrument for government'.

Although we only actually meet Rudolf Hess as a character within the narrative, succinct comments are made about the main Nazi protagonists. According to reliable accounts, Hitler was 'boring', Himmler was 'a prude', Goerring was 'a snob', Goebbels was 'withdrawn' and Hess was a 'vegetarian crank'. Later von Bek revises his opinion of the Führer, describing him as 'deeply banal and profoundly mad'. He knows that the Nazi salute is a poor copy of the Roman salute used in the film *Quo Vadis*, and in the end he almost pities Hitler for being a small man out of his depth.

Ulric von Bek is visited by two characters from Moorcock's roll-call, Prince Gaynor and Klosterheim, who demand that von Bek hand over his sword, Ravenbrand. Prince Gaynor, Corum's old adversary, was introduced in *The Queen of the Swords* and reappeared against Elric in *The Revenge of the Rose*, while the sinister figure of Klosterheim continues to be von Bek's eternal adversary. Their appearance in *The Dreamthief's Daughter* begins a supernatural adventure, as we learn that Gaynor is merely using the Nazi uniform to tap into a greater and more ancient force. Hitler's rise to power is only a microcosm or an echo of a larger story being played out on many planes concurrently. Von Bek gets caught up in a nightmarish chase through the mythical land of Mittelmarch, the borderlands between the human world and Faerie — a place similar to the Nordic Alfheim, or Elfland. Moorcock previously used Mittelmarch as a location in *The City in the Autumn Stars*.

Professor of English, David Punter, remarks in his book on Gothic fantasy, *The Literature of Terror, Volume 2,* how 'Moorcock especially demonstrates a considerable power in the manipulation of mythic and quasi-mythic materials', and in *The Dreamthief's Daughter,* the author startlingly and successfully manipulates ancient Egyptian, Celtic, Arthurian and Teutonic mythologies into a story of Wagnerian proportions that intertwines with Moorcock's own multiverse of Tanelorn and the Eternal Champion, creating a contemporary myth.

In 1930s Germany von Bek is taken to Sachsenhausen prison camp where his brutal torture is described with a distant and indifferent voice. Von Bek's dispassionate narration adds to the general horror the reader already feels towards the Nazis and their abuse of power. Eventually, of course, the reliable League of Temporal Adventurers, including Oswald Bastable, help von Bek to escape and divert him towards his fate of fighting for the balance.

It transpires that von Bek is a version of Elric in a parallel world, and through the dreams that have been directed by Oona, the dreamthief's daughter, the two champions merge to become 'two men in a single body' for about seventy pages of the novel. It seems that dreams are merely glimpses of these other lives and balance is restored when we move between these lives and change them. The true plot then unravels as the Eternal Champion fights with Gaynor the Damned; chaos against law.

Once again, Moorcock plays with names, and in a moment of postmodern satire he calls one of the decrepit, insane goddesses of law, Duchess Miggea, an anagram of Maggie (Margaret Thatcher) and one of the ineffective knights (with a wide grin) is named Baron Blare (Tony Blair). Moonglum, the eternal companion, reappears, and one cannot help but wonder if Oona is a version of Una Persson, who is often the companion of Oswald Bastable. Links are frequently made to the connected novel, *The Fortress of the Pearl,* in which Elric meets Oona's mother.

The Dreamthief's Daughter becomes a quest for the elusive and inconstant Holy Grail, which we are told can transform into any object, such as a sword or even a person. The champions then travel the unpredictable moonbeam roads to find a realm known as 'the Grey Fees', which are made up of 'the fundamental stuff of the multiverse', the life force itself, created by human memory and desire: as if imagination and will had become matter. 'Grey Fees', we are told, is actually a corruption of Grail Fields, and thus the quest comes full circle as Elric and von Bek attempt to stop Gaynor from becoming a new and corrupt god. Power, in many of Moorcock's novels, is symbolised by a talisman, and his favourite is that of the Arthurian legend. The Holy Grail was originally the chalice from which Christ drank at the last supper, and for Moorcock it comes to represent the Balance itself. Power also resides in swords, coming from another Arthurian legend — that of Excalibur. Charlemagne had his sword and Roland blew his horn, Olivant, and Moorcock, like many fantasists, employs symbols to represent supernatural and archaic power.

The novel's grand finale gives a new twist to the Battle of Britain and echoes the typical Moorcockian climax on the scale of Götterdämmerung. Normality is restored and von Bek is left to evaluate the effect not only on his homeland but on the entire multiverse. However, by the end of the novel he has still not found the Grail or his lost son.

The Dreamthief's Daughter leaves the reader with a challenging remark about British culture in the twenty-first century; von Bek assesses the state of England, once great with its poets and historians, but now decadent and in entropy 'because she no longer possessed men of such integrity and breadth of vision'. The task of the Eternal Champion is to rise above the general malaise and apathy of our lazy culture and to make a real difference in the lives that we lead and the actions that we choose to take. In the words of von Bek: 'It seemed we were all fated to live identical lives in billions of counter-realities rarely able to change our stories yet constantly striving to do so. Occasionally one of us was successful.'

Although Elric has become a demigod, a warrior who rescues humanity from the grip of evil, what *The Dreamthief's Daughter* really demonstrates is that the true champions are 'the invisible people' — the normal men and women of our own world and time, or as Oswald Bastable explains to von Bek: 'The ordinary heroes and heroines of these appalling conflicts between corrupted Chaos and degenerate Law.' Perhaps we are all avatars of the Eternal Champion, needing to understand our own fate to enable us to fight for the balance within our individual lives and for society.

Subtitled 'The Albino in America', *The Skrayling Tree* (2003) uncovers Moorcock's interest in Native American mythology, which adds a different gloss to his usual multiversal musings. The role of the eternal companion is taken by Hiawatha, a loquacious and well-educated individual, who, like the protagonists, is also seeking his own destiny through a dream quest. He is able to explain that 'skraelings' (meaning 'screamers') was the name given to native Indians — because of the noises they made. As ever, Moorcock invokes the stretching of parameters: 'To think in terms of linear time is to be time's slave.' And: 'The multiverse depended upon chance and malleable realities.' This means that characters can meet themselves, change size and scale and move between planes and intersecting realities. White Crow is an intriguing character — an albino shaman astride a woolly mammoth called Bess, who becomes a delightful character in her own right.

Our heroes travel through a land of magic and elemental spirits, slowly learning that 'the action of every individual affects the whole'. Oona, Elric and Ulric gradually make their way to the eponymous Skrayling Tree, which, as the sum of all our souls, somehow holds the secrets of the entire multiverse. Oona is kidnapped and Ulric goes in search of his wife, while Elric, who has been fighting in the Crusades, eventually sails with Vikings to pre-Columbian America. There he meets the suave and sophisticated Prince Lobkowitz, who works for the Balance. Lobkowitz is an existentialist and arguably embodies the philosophies of Moorcock himself. He tells von Bek: 'I believe that if God exists he has given us the power of creativity and has left us with it. If we did not exist, it would be necessary for him to create us. While he neither judges nor plans, he has given us the Balance.'

Von Bek, meanwhile, is guided by the black giant, Sepiriz, who reunites him with the sword Ravenbrand, after which there ensues an almighty battle to save the multiverse. This conflict between Law and Chaos is more complex than mere good versus evil, as von Bek reminds us: 'The Balance offered creativity and justice — a combination of all human qualities in harmony.' Now that seems like something worth fighting for.

There is something here to keep all Moorcock enthusiasts happy. The book contains landscapes 'of the most appalling beauty, of elaborate horror and hideous symmetry' (such as 'foaming rivers of dust'). There are also the usual array of intertextual jokes and references for the avid reader. Throwaway references are made to Erekosë, Ilian of Garathorm, Rose and a pirate called Kwelch. The author namechecks a school in Sussex he attended as a child and even calls one chapter 'The Hawk Wind'. There are also literary and artistic allusions to Blake, Hardy, Pushkin and Bruegel. Like those artists, Moorcock views things on a grand and epic scale, in which the individual is witnessed in an individual struggle against the impossible cruelties of nature and fate. The Eternal Champion learns that self-deception is what often holds us back from redemption.

Ending the trilogy is *The White Wolf's Son* (2005), narrated by Oonagh von Bek, granddaughter of Oona. Pursued by Gaynor and Klosterheim, Oonagh is helped by the likes of Bastable, Lord Reynard the Fox and a certain writer and his wife, Linda, who live in Texas. Even Glogauer gets a namecheck, while the presence of John Daker from the Erekosë books completes and connects the entire cycle.

In the Middle March where 'All realities meet', they find a blind albino boy called Onric — Elric's son — yet this novel is closely tied to the Hawkmoon series, with references to the Runestaff and descriptions of 'Londra' where King Huon, the 'wizened homunculus', rules from his womb-like throne. As Moorcock's classic Eternal Champion adventures, this also ends with a spectacular cosmic battled played out in the heavens. Summing up his extended metaphor the author gets his characters to explain — as if for the last time — the balance. Una Persson, our guide through the multiverse, reminds us: 'One way lies madness and hideous death; the other sanity and relentless nothingness.' Then Elric — surely the ultimate champion — comes to a sober conclusion about this personal dualistic struggle: 'Even our most private thoughts and yearnings, he suspected, were dictated by some preordained scenario in which Law battled Chaos. The best we could hope for was a brief respite from their eternal war.'

Another novel about the ubiquitous von Beks requiring brief discussion is *The Brothel In Rosenstrasse* (1982), which examines the theme of European conflict, this time at the end of the nineteenth century. Moorcock sets the novel in Mirenburg, the capital of Waldenstein — a location so realistic that it gets readers reaching for their atlases. Mirenburg is on the brink of a civil war, threatened with destruction, while the novel's protagonist, Count von Bek, muses how 'man's greatest monuments, his architecture, never outlast his acts of aggression'.

The Brothel in Rosenstrasse begins with a history of Mirenburg, an idealised Bohemia, giving the novel its vivid identity and sense of place. It seems Mirenburg owes something to such cities as Prague and Vienna. Mirenburg is probably also a version of Tanelorn, the resting place of the Eternal Champion.

The second part of *The Brothel in Rosenstrasse* details the sexual appetites of the brothel's upper class patrons, who, in the third part, are disturbed by the political upheaval brought about by revolutionary terrorism. This intense novel details the decadent lives of the prosperous classes in the decadent setting of Frau Schmetterling's brothel, which comes to symbolise an old world order of sensuality and epicureanism. The eroticism retains a dignity and is described with a sense of aesthetic taste by the voice of a connoisseur, exposing Moorcock's own familiarity with brothels. In fact, sexuality becomes a political metaphor for the changing power in Eastern Europe; sex is more important than love, and old von Bek and his sixteen-year-old lover can never be compatible. Count von Bek is selfish and unsympathetic throughout. The brothel itself is a microcosm of elegance, like Mirenburg, Gothic and subject to ancient laws. Neither, however, can stand up to the violence of modern warfare. The self-indulgence of the powerful classes spoils the intimacy of relationships, illuminating how greed and selfishness, like war, are destructive to individuals and societies both.

10: LONDON
'THE INCIDENTS IN *MOTHER LONDON* PARALLEL MY OWN RECOLLECTIONS OF THE WAR VERY CLOSELY.'

The symphonic novel *Mother London* (1988) is a celebration of Moorcock's home. It explores the history of the twentieth century and expresses the individual anxiety and struggle for identity within the modern city. Mostly, however, it is about London herself... and London is the protagonist of the novel. As the author states: 'London — thanks in a large part to her writers — has always been the richest, most coherent, civilised, tolerant and inspiring cosmopolitan megapolis in the world.' *Mother London* is an epic project, masterfully executed and, according to the author, his magnum opus. Many critics agreed. The novelist Angela Carter reviewed Moorcock's book in *The Guardian* with great enthusiasm, praising it as 'a vast, uncorseted, sentimental, comic, elegiac salmagundi of a novel,' while American reviewer Paul Witcover hailed it as 'an authentic work of genius.' *Mother London* was shortlisted for the Whitbread Prize.

Moorcock evokes 'place' in his novels with some eloquence. He created the decadent city of Mirenburg in *The Brothel in Rosenstrasse* and Gloriana's Albion remains his elegy to the historical London, but in *Mother London* he celebrates the modern city, which has become a sentient, conscious character. Moorcock's London becomes more than a single place, containing within itself a complete realm of mythology — a multiverse.

As an icon the city fulfils many functions, such as that of a labyrinth full of dark secrets, a mother protecting her offspring, a destructive asylum of anxiety and control, and finally a living creature. The people and the city are symbiotic, for there is no city without inhabitants and those who live there are shaped in turn by the place. London is a mother, although not necessarily a benevolent one. The city speaks through the pain and passion of her children, like a Greek chorus. This is a truly polyphonic novel, narrated by a number of different voices and viewpoints.

Mother London follows a complex structure, a non-chronological pattern which undulates like a tide. Unusually, the climax occurs in the middle with horrific descriptions of the Blitz, leaving a gradual and anti-climactic ending. Motifs are developed and themes are revisited throughout the novel, and this non-linear and seemingly random collage makes it a surreal picture of London and its history. The city landscape and its inhabitants are explored through an episodic narrative carefully placed around the chorus of the city's collective consciousness.

Moorcock allows us three narrative perspectives — David, Josef and Mary, three outpatients at the same psychiatric clinic. Each represents a facet of Moorcock himself. The most clearly autobiographical chapters are those narrated in the first person by David Mummery, a name referring to the medieval folk performer, the mummer, and implying a hypocritical or theatrical display. Mummery's first name has religious significance, connecting him with Christ (often called the Son of David), thereby completing the trinity of Mary (a resurrected spirit and mother) and Josef (a father figure).

Mummery describes himself as an urban anthropologist, a role also undertaken by Moorcock in the writing of this novel. Such narrative complexity can be seen in Jungian terms, whereby Moorcock's ego/self is divided into three main archetypes or masks: Mummery is the child, symbolising the whole self, Mary is the anima, and Josef is both the wise man and the fool. Each facet of the author reflects a specific interest: Mummery's perspective is autobiographical and of a personal London; Josef stands for a nostalgic era and represents the life force of the indigenous

Londoner; Mary lives in the dreamworld of a mythological London. All three Londons are real and all overlap.

David Mummery, who represents the young Moorcock, is the most enigmatic character. *Mother London* is an introverted and personal novel containing streams-of-consciousness and mystic vision. Other than *Letters from Hollywood*, Moorcock's attempts at autobiography have been fictionalised and unreliable, while Moorcock openly admits that Glogauer, Elric and Jerry Cornelius represent aspects of himself. Mummery is likewise self-deprecating and infernally melancholic, brooding and self-indulgent, a familiar trait of both Elric and Cornelius.

One of Moorcock's earliest memories was watching the Blitz over South London, just as is described by David Mummery, with the war-torn ruins becoming a childhood playground. In one interview, Moorcock described this formative childhood experience: 'I grew up in a constantly altered landscape... but it wasn't frightening to children of my age. There was an enormous amount of freedom involved.' Like Mummery, Moorcock was also expelled from an experimental school in East Sussex, had an uncle who was a civil servant living at 10 Downing Street, and played in a skiffle band called the Greenhorns.

Another chapter linked directly to Moorcock's own experience describes the police brutality and racism at the Notting Hill Carnival in 1977. The narrator, Mummery, has inside information that the police and 'white residents' of Notting Hill have formulated a plan to start a riot so that future carnivals would be banned. This frightening scenario concurs with Moorcock's account in his political tract *The Retreat From Liberty* (1983), a discussion of the erosion of civil rights in contemporary Britain. In this polemic Moorcock describes another moment during the carnival, which later became a scene in *Mother London*: 'At one point a friend sat in a predominantly black cafe while a line of policemen banged their truncheons on their riot shields by way of challenge. Inside, he said, everyone kept their cool and ignored the police... The blacks maintained their apparent insouciance while the natives outside tried to break their nerves with displays of aggression.'

Notting Hill Gate in the sixties and seventies was an eclectic, decadent and mystical environment full of folklore and conflict and there is no doubt that living there heavily affected Moorcock's personal and political outlook. His warning conclusion in *The Retreat from Liberty* is one that is also explored in much of his fiction: 'Whether we are destroyed by a process of social collapse or by the explosion of nuclear missiles the fault will lie ultimately with us — in our own capacity for self-deception and our unwillingness to deal directly and courageously with the realities and injustices of our daily lives.'

Josef represents a more mature Moorcock, suave and romantic. Like David and Mary he is a psychiatric patient who can hear voices, using his telepathic skill in the war to rescue trapped victims. He is a hero who manages to seduce, save lives and converse with a demon, but we also witness him visiting a prostitute and making a drunken, naked spectacle of himself. He is a Falstaffian character who, in an inspired moment of naïve insanity, manages to miraculously defuse a bomb and save lives. The description is closer to Don Quixote than Achilles: 'With a gasp, almost a sob, he rammed the shears into the works and snipped. He snipped twice more, trusting to whatever instincts he had... then snipped again as the bile rose in his mouth and he felt he would drown in it... It grumbled, whimpered and grew silent.' Josef attempts to find a balance between the chaos of his psychic powers and his own need for order: 'His routine and his own particular medicine are his protection against chaos.' Josef faces physical and mental chaos and manages to survive what Moorcock implies were two of the most destructive forces of the twentieth century — World War

II and Thatcherism.

The decades present us with changing cultures. The fifties are austere, the sixties exciting and avant-garde, but the seventies see the beginning of entropy. Moorcock frequently celebrates the sixties, but like many has come to realise that this romantic view is also a somewhat unreal one.

Moorcock continues to comment on British culture through other characters, many of whom show cynical reactions to the so-called hippy revolution. For example, Patsy Meakin, a minor character, an avant-garde filmmaker, uses the spirit of the age to his own advantage: 'The counterculture had taken Patsy by surprise and only received his interest because of the pretty girls it attracted... If it promised the joys of teenage dolly birds, good drugs, and the chance of an orgy or two, he was willing to look a bit of a twit.' Moorcock suggests this may have been a prevalent view.

Josef blames what he calls the 'Thatcher-belt' for ruining the real London. 'You hear them moaning about the people who were born there as if those were the interlopers! It's classic imperialism.' Josef's fear is that London will become a theme park, such as Dickensland, and this fear is realised when David's cousin George outlines his plans to open The New Ludgate Chop House on the site of The Old King Lud pub. Lud was the founder and protector of London, a Celtic god of great importance to history, myth and fantasy, and it seems ludicrous that he has become the inspiration for a plastic theme-restaurant. Mary sees this as an inevitable process of the self-mythologisation of civilisation, but Josef rejects this.

The Scaramanga sisters, whom Josef saves, represent a more rural, nostalgic, village life, which has been swallowed up by Greater London. They live in a cottage by the canal with barges at the end of the garden, and drink tea from china cups, but their haven is ruined by the Blitz: 'All the insects, all the butterflies and birds were gone, as in a fairy tale.' It is as if something beautiful has been destroyed; London, like some Garden of Eden, has been spoiled by man's pride and greed.

Josef's visions are the most vivid. During the Blitz he witnesses an apocalyptic hallucination of the city coming to life, rousing 'the sleeping gods of London'. He sees angels and giants from the city's mythology, hears the voices of all the inhabitants, and is aware of 'his voice joining the millions to form a single monumental howl'. As in Moorcock's early sword and sorcery novels, angels and demons continue to symbolise a more personal battle, and internal conflict is projected onto the larger canvasses of world politics and even Heaven and Hell. After the war, Josef continues having supernatural experiences, which he relates as normal events: 'I was walking there… when I ran slap into a demon.' Josef's vision during the Blitz reads like a description of the hordes of chaos in one of the author's earlier fantasies.

Mary is a more ambiguous character. Her grasp on reality is incomplete — she remains in a dream world of Hollywood glamour and surreal fantasy. Mary, like London, is a mother who has survived the war, but has trouble coping with the modern world. Waking from a coma she hears voices and seems to have second sight, but the voices are often brutal and pornographic.

It is during 1970 that Mary, Josef and David find the greatest fulfilment. It is a moment of perfect happiness on a fairground merry-go-round. All the characters agree 'they would gladly live this instant forever'. Acid has enabled some kind of mystical 'multiversal vision' and the colour and wonder of the fairground is augmented by the gathered hippies: 'in afghans and bell-bottoms and flowers they call themselves the children of the sun.' In contrast to Josef's demonic vision, it is a glimpse of paradise and a utopian end time.

Back in 1975, Moorcock and his band the Deep Fix released

New Worlds Fair, a concept album about a fairground which becomes the last place in a world which is dissipating. Songs such as Last Merry Go Round and Dodgem Dude follow the dangerous rides and false dreams. The fairground is a sinister place where customers experience both pleasure and fear, and become lost in a fake haze of movement, smells and sensuality. It is an ersatz world, full of corruption and profit, in which the rust is covered by a veneer of paint and the customer is hypnotised and momentarily beguiled. It is interesting that in *Mother London* the characters are happiest at this moment. All their problems are forgotten and each has become an innocent child, distracted from all the tragedy that has befallen them. All their friends join them on the final ride, which seems to endlessly repeat itself. This moment of ecstasy is orgiastic, the jouissance unendingly repeated, and from the merry-go-round David cries a human and rather pathetic plea: 'Don't let it ever stop.' Perhaps escaping reality — fantasy itself — is the only answer.

The novel ends with the figure of Old Non, a wandering tramp, whose name is an anagram of London. She knows all the legends about Gog and Magog, the giants guarding London; about Bran the Celtic giant, whose head is buried under Parliament Hill; of all the ghosts of the Bloody Tower; of Dick Turpin and Dan Leno. Moorcock's comforting, authorial voice reminds the reader of the value of fantasy. 'By means of our myths and legends we maintain a sense of what we are worth and who we are. Without them we should undoubtedly go mad.'

London, home to millions, is herself growing senile and is personified by the dotty, homeless storyteller, who wanders the streets, sharing her wisdom like the last surviving Wyrd Sister, keeping alive the ancient mysteries and eternal wonders of the city. By giving one subtle reference, Moorcock completes his own multiverse by having Josef refer to Old Non at one point as 'Mrs C'.

This has huge implications with regard to Moorcock's complicated internal referencing, because Mrs C is Jerry Cornelius' mother. It is difficult to discern the seriousness of Moorcock's intention; being unpredictable he may just be teasing readers — or making an important statement. Mrs C certainly fulfils a universal role similar to London, and if Jerry is Everyman then there is no difficulty in following the argument that his coarse, senile but loveable mum is, in a multiversal sense, also the mother of us all. This may be the author's joke.

Even if London has failed to realise Blake's vision, as Josef we must also cling to the hope that humanity is essentially good. This is Moorcock's romantic notion. 'London endures. Her stories endure. People's demand for Romance endures. And I retain confidence in human nature.'

Just like Albion in *Gloriana*, London contains the 'inner landscapes' of memory, dreams and the 'collective unconscious'. The irony is that the protagonists are deemed 'mad', but as readers we are shown that true madness comes with war, destroying all that is dear to us: our families, our identity, and our own home. *Mother London* is a complex novel about love, loss and redemption in which the city becomes a metaphor for faith and salvation. The real London is, of course, the one in your mind.

King of the City (2000) is again set in London, although there is less of a sense of the city as a sentient character, and more straightforward nostalgia — which cannot always be taken at face value. *King of the City* may well be more autobiographical, and it certainly updates the history of London, which ended at 1985 in *Mother London*. Unlike its predecessor, *King of the City* escapes beyond the realm of London, trespassing on foreign soils such as Rwanda and Kosovo, places mired in conflict at the time the novel was written.

The structure of the novel is once again unorthodox. The

first half of the book describes vignettes of popular London life, punctuated with anti-capitalist political polemics; a conventional plot only begins after the first 200 pages. Writer Iain Sinclair accurately described the novel as 'a comprehensive encyclopaedia of lost lives, uncelebrated loci, trashed cultural memory'.

Its tone is decidedly existentialist, set by the anti-conservative voice of the narrator, Dennis Dover, who pessimistically sums up the twentieth century: 'You start with the first concentration camps, an Imperial war, carving up Africa, add a chorus of all the agonised millions calling from the dirt of no man's land, into the Russian Civil War, the Chinese Civil War, the Spanish Civil War, Stalin, the rise of Fascism, the Holocaust, World War Two, Hiroshima, Korea, Vietnam, Cambodia, Afghanistan, Iraq and Bosnia, Rwanda and East Timor. And Kosovo of course... What a bloody century.' When seen from this realistic perspective, Moorcock leaves the reader wondering exactly what we have learned from the lessons of history.

The first and last lines of the novel echo each other and emphasise the themes of 'myths and miracles', subjects familiar to all fantasy readers. However, this novel is set in a very real and recognisable present-day, with the first person narration using slang, expletives and street talk. Dennis, or Den, a paparazzo photojournalist and rock star, is once more an aspect of Michael Moorcock himself, writer, traveller and leader of the band the Deep Fix. Den's early experience of playing guitar at a gig echoes Elric's wielding of the black blade, Stormbringer: 'My Rickenbacker was bucking out of my control, screaming with complicated lusts, radiating funny black light. Its strings were silver rays piercing infinity. Roadways through the multiverse.' He later plays a guitar called a Black Falcon that gives 'the sense of you being the guitar and the guitar being you'.

In fact, just like *Mother London*, there are three main characters, all of whom reflect a persona of the author. Den's foil is Rosie Beck, his cousin, with whom he is in love and who, like an aspect of the Eternal Champion, spends her life helping the victims of poverty, war and injustice.

Barbican Begg, a multi-millionaire, best represents the spirit of free enterprise against whom Rosie and Den are sworn to struggle, although their ways are, at times, dubious. As the millionaire continues to destroy London herself, Den develops a deeper resentment, feeling that his 'roots were being chopped off'. Once again, Moorcock shows capitalism as the enemy of community and personal identity.

A recognisable character from Moorcock's cast of regulars is Al Rikh, a mysterious but powerful albino sheikh. There are also a number of real people involved, such as Hawkwind singer and poet Robert Calvert, as well as most of the Hawkwind and Deep Fix members. For example, an important character in *King of the City* is Tubby Ollis, whose real name is Dorian Theakston, and the drummers listed on the two Deep Fix albums are D. Theaker and Terry Ollis (also of Hawkwind). Tubby is an agent of chaos fighting bigotry and politicians (or at least pitching custard pies in their direction), and the sub-plot concerning the defence of his mill is one of the most vivid episodes in the novel.

Den's discussion of British rock music is anecdotal and realistic, referring to names such as David Bowie, Alex Harvey, and Annie Lennox, even claiming that 'the job in The Police was between me and Andy Summers'. Later on, Den cringes at the thought that he was nearly in a band with Bill Clinton and Tony Blair. As *King of the City* develops, it becomes Moorcock's personal fantasy in which his alter-ego, Den, makes a comeback with Deep Fix and becomes 'suddenly more famous than Michael Jackson'. They appear on TV's *Top of the Pops*, get a single banned from US radio, and perform a gig on Tower Bridge before Princess Diana and an all-star audience, relayed by satellite television across the world.

Cynical of British political and mainstream culture, Denny enjoys making sarcastic remarks about prime ministers 'Margaret Hatchet' and 'Tony Blurr' — 'Mrs T used the language of liberal humanism to reinstall feudalism.' Like many he sees New Labour as continuing the policies of Margaret Thatcher. In the latter part of the novel, he gets drawn into some of the horrors in Kosovo, experiencing personal tragedy that leads to suicidal paranoia. But it is through recognising the terrible and tragic mistakes of the twentieth century that mankind could finally learn the simple truth. 'That common dream. That place of peace and good health we were promised as the prize of our progress.' The only hope lies not in consumerism, capitalism or fascism, but in the ideals of what anarchist philosopher Peter Kropotkin called 'mutual aid'. Den comforts himself with a similar vision: 'a mutually respecting civil and civilised world, judging itself by its best ideas and actions.'

He eventually gets a second chance to reinvent himself, find love and see the world through new eyes. Rosie's conspiracy has created a revolution that will make the world a better place and she is identified as the true Eternal Champion — or perhaps she is the controller of the balance who can manipulate people and history. Den is eventually king of a new city of hope and ideals, and this is the miracle — that London can once more become 'the best and most progressive, the richest and greatest city the world has ever known'. But happiness comes not with money and fame — it can only be found through love. The miracle of peace and justice may only be a myth, but never underestimate the power of myth and fantasy. Moorcock has developed his own multiversal myth further and his moral is optimistic; where would we be without the power to dream?

Moorcock himself is the king of the multiverse, or of his London at least. (Publication for *King of the City* coincided with the election for London Mayor and the publicity posters announced, 'Vote for Michael Moorcock.') The entire novel is a celebratory monologue for the city that is his real home, and the author manipulates London just as Elric wields the symbiotic sword, Stormbringer. Even if Michael Moorcock now lives in Texas, his heart and soul must surely remain in London.

Jonathan Raban, in his anthropological study, *Soft City*, examines the fluctuating reality of urban life, describing the city as a theatrical mirage where lives are scenarios and strangers an audience. Raban praises the city's ambiguity and shallow veneer: 'London was pure make-believe, a city I could belong to because I could invent it.' Raban writes particularly about Notting Hill Gate and Ladbroke Grove, where Moorcock lived for many years; home and preferred enclave of Jerry Cornelius and Colonel Pyat; reigned over by Gloriana; and even a battleground for the Runestaff.

Raban refers to the mythology of Notting Hill Gate, where folk-magic still exists in the guise of drugs, music, decadence, astrology, mysticism and art. Ladbroke Grove is famous for producing writers and musicians, such as Hawkwind and the Pink Fairies. It was also the home of *International Times* and Jimi Hendrix. Raban recognises the importance of identifying the 'soft' city, which is ambiguous and in flux. Our material world comes alive when it interacts with our dreams and illusions, and surrealistic art begins to communicate that reality. The city is soft like Dalì's watches or Cornelius' sense of time, people and place.

Raban likens city fashions to theatrical costumes and compares life in the city to acting on a stage: 'In the city, we can change our identities at will, as Dickens triumphantly proved over and over again in his fiction... The gaudy theatrical nature of the city itself tends constantly to melodrama.'

The city is a venue for melodrama, an underrated theatrical form that is both amoral and anarchistic, as Raban shows, and shares many features with an earlier age of magic and barbarism. Cities contain tribes, rituals, superstition, territories, violence, magic and folklore. Raban suggests that the city is a place rich in mythology and fantasy. He explains how 'we have created an environment in which it is exceedingly hard to be rational, in which people are turning to magic as a natural first resort'. The city is a surreal cartoon, or in Raban's words, 'a maniac's scrapbook', and Moorcock is that maniac, pasting down the collage of his experiences and observations.

11: EXPANDING THE MULTIVERSE
'NOTHING IN MY BOOKS IS WITHOUT PURPOSE.'

Now resident in Texas, Moorcock continues to develop his ever-expanding multiverse. His triptych of novels known as The Second Ether is not properly a trilogy, although marketed as such. Like many of Moorcock's novels, they claim to be manuscripts written by someone else — in this case they are the property of Edwin Begg. *Blood* (1994) is an experimental novel compiled from previously published episodes; *Fabulous Harbours* (1995) is a collection of related stories about various Beks and Beggs; leaving *The War Amongst the Angels* (1996) as a sequel to *Blood*. Set in a future alternative Mississippi, the four central characters in *Blood* are experienced gamblers in the Game of Time or 'la zeitjuego'. These players can make decisions which affect their own destinies and the novel investigates the existential notion of having the freedom to choose your own future, and in doing so, affect the whole multiverse.

Equilibrium in a disordered world is achieved with pseudo-mathematics, through playing a type of virtual reality game involving the symbiosis of player and character. The 'Chaos Engineers' are comic strip heroes from a typical space-opera pulp magazine, although Moorcock never allows the reader to be completely certain of this; but the episodes with Captain Billy-Bob Begg and his corsairs fighting the evil 'Original Insect' soon become a postmodern pastiche of irony and self-reference with their adventures woven into the main narrative. These 'jugadors' are able to 'fold' through time and space to the second ether to begin the true game, which is 'a struggle between life and death'. The game is psychic, involving the disembodied consciousness floating through ether, but only when spirit is combined with physical reality (blood) is fulfilment accomplished.

The ambiguous protagonist, the Rose (who is part flora, part human) first appeared in *The Revenge of the Rose* (1991) and is a character in Moorcock's dramatis personae with whom he has a particular empathy. She is not only a member of the ever-growing von Bek clan, but, we are told, is the author's own fictional cousin. In *Blood*, she alone seems to be enlightened enough to express hope: 'The world is full of more wisdom than destructive ignorance... Why can't that vast majority of us band together to achieve peace and equity?' This echoes Moorcock's anarchistic ideals of 'mutual aid'.

Once again Moorcock writes on a grand scale. *The War Amongst the Angels* culminates in Armageddon but Moorcock manages to provide metaphysics with little moralising. The familiar Moorcockian pantheon fights the final battle for the balance, echoing many of the finales of his sword and sorcery tales. This time, however, there is a difference. A casual footnote, from the author, states: 'The War in Heaven had long since ceased to be between God and the Devil. Now it was between a myriad different interests, each increasingly losing sight of its original goals in a series of pointlessly cynical alliances.' Those interests are still represented by the dualism of chaos and law, except now the terms have been refined and informed by the author's reading of chaos theory so that chaos becomes 'plurality', and law 'singularity'.

Echoing Moorcock's epic scope, chaos theory views the world macrocosmically rather than in the quantum terms of particles and quarks. Popular science writer James Gleick identified the importance of the following question for chaos theorists: 'In a universe ruled by entropy, drawing inexorably toward greater and greater disorder, how does order arise?' This same question is one that has obsessed Moorcock for more than fifty years.

When interviewed, Moorcock is explicit about his references in *Blood*: 'Chaos theory is a distinct help in that it provides a logic system, which means you can develop fiction more readily. The more tools you've got the more you can structure something. Chaos theory has helped me enormously with that.' Chaos theory claims to see patterns emerge within scientific irregularities, or as Gleick expresses it, 'Life sucks order from a sea of disorder.'

In the near future of *Blood* the world has become unstable due to the natural entropic pull, causing ultra-reality to leak violently from the Biloxi Fault, while time is now measured by 'degrees of deliquescence'. Entropy inevitably leads to a gradual dissipation into nothingness as a natural state, but Moorcock's work also offers an alternative to entropy. Love and life-affirming sexuality can replace drained energy and allow individuals to rediscover or recreate their identities, empowering them to travel the moonbeam paths of the multiverse to a new time or plane of existence.

Moorcock tackles metaphysical questions and the Rose states their true aim: 'We're playing for the power to change the human condition.' Moorcock's presentation of God is always as a benign and absent abstraction; the closest he gets to an identify is as 'the Great Mood'. He does, however, use the scientific concept of fractals to explain how we are smaller versions of infinity or 'echoes of some lost original'.

It remains for us to entertain ourselves and play our hand with the greatest skill. Life is a gamble and a gambol, or a comic book, and the characters in The Second Ether series are creating worlds as much as Moorcock is himself. They appear to become the characters in the game they are playing, leaving the edges between play and reality blurred and ambivalent, creating a postmodern Möbius strip of never-ending layers. We are left frantically searching for meaning in our chaotic voyages across malleable landscapes, adrift in a steamboat or dirigible heading towards the 'Biloxi Fault'.

Moorcock has also been enticed into returning to his comic book beginnings and from November 1997 DC published twelve successful monthly comic editions called *Michael Moorcock's Multiverse,* scripted by the author himself. The comic merges stories of the Rose, Elric and a reincarnation of Sexton Blake, Sir Seaton Begg, an Eternal Champion distantly related to von Bek. The story 'Moonbeams and Roses' recasts some of the characters from *Blood.*

The comics add further understanding to the concept of the multiverse, which, we are told, is made up of 'countless versions of the old stories which we learn from our dreams, which are echoed by our own stories, which are, in turn, retold... and which we are sometimes able to change'. The Rose is given great prominence, as she is in *The War Amongst the Angels.* She is the Eternal Champion — 'I have one personality and a million selves' — and as such is 'sworn to bring coherence out of chaos and chaos out of stagnation'.

Once again, in the comics, Moorcock raises and develops his favourite themes, enabling us to dream of exotic adventures wherein that romantic spirit of chaos eternally defeats the dull, predictable and soulless singularity of Reason.

The three stories are interlinked and merge together in the final issue as Count Zodiac (an albino), Begg and a certain Jerry Cornelius unify into one champion while Elric confronts King Silverskin, who is every aspect of the Eternal Champion. By absorbing Silverskin, Elric creates 'an unrepeatable moment of absolute harmony — a single chance of redemption for the entire multiverse'. It is the Rose, however, who finally defeats the evil amalgamation of Prince Gaynor the Damned (who has previously confronted Corum and Elric) and Paul Minct (who appeared in *Blood).*

The comics are also a chance for Moorcock to make cross-references to earlier novels such as *The Brothel in Rosenstrasse*, to resurrect popular characters such as Moonglum, the eternal companion, and also to develop his own self-referencing. In 'Moonbeams and Roses', not only is Moorcock himself a player and observer at the Terminal Café, but he is joined by the artist Walter Simonson. More comic series have since followed.

Silverheart (2000), Moorcock's collaboration with fellow fantasy writer Storm Constantine, is subtitled *A Novel of the Multiverse* and introduces a new champion, Max Silverskin, whose surname links him both with the *MMM* comics and the new Elric novels.

When asked about the practicalities of co-writing a novel, Moorcock is more than willing to give details. He explained his working relationship with Storm Constantine in the following way: 'I was originally asked to provide a scenario for a [computer] game... Once we'd agreed the basic idea I sat down and began a scenario so detailed that it became a short novel of some 45,000 words... It's pretty much a good fifty-fifty collaboration, with Storm adding characteristic elements.' Constantine cites Michael Moorcock as her main inspiration as an adolescent fantasy reader.

As a novel *Silverheart* is not wholly satisfying, suffering from the trite quest and unnecessary fighting obligatory to the gaming format. The protagonist, Max Silverskin, searches for objects and travels through magical realms, making it a fascinating idea for the computer animator and game-player, but something of a clichéd novel.

Even if it is not written solely by Moorcock, *Silverheart* contains a multitude of Moorcockian signatures and devices. The introduction is written by 'Cornelius Begg', amalgamating two Moorcock characters, and the female protagonist is once again another incarnation of the Rose. The theme is that of the balance of chaos and order, and the novel ends with Moorcock's traditional epiphany and reconciliation.

The novel introduces The Council of the Metal, which, with its unchanging orthodoxy and medieval feudal class system, runs the city of Karadur. Law and order is represented by Captain Coffin and his secret police and is symbolised by the Gragonatt Fortress, from which Max Silverskin, thief and folk-hero, escapes by supernatural means. A mysterious voice challenges Max to 'Discover what you are or may be', which is surely a philosophical quest for each and every one of us.

Max discovers Karadur's parallel city, Shriltasi, a land of magic ('barishi') that was separated after the Reformation, which like our own Enlightenment in eighteenth century Europe, looked down on all that was not scientific and logical. Max's adventures begin to make more sense once he meets the Ashen folk and some of his own relatives, from whom he learns to control his magical powers. He begins to question his social programming and learn to feel beyond the limiting human senses. Rose discovers that 'tradition is a blindfold' and Serenia Silverskin teaches her son, Max, that 'death is not a thing to be feared' and that the safest passage is 'the middle path. Extremes of any kind are to be avoided'.

Rose goes against her own father, Lord Iron, ruler of the Council of Metal, whose belief is: 'Millennia have taught us never to change our customs.' Max slowly comes to a realisation: 'The Lords of the Metal didn't just control Karadur, they controlled reality. They wrote the history books, determining what was true and false. They castigated innovative thought, so that even the most intelligent citizens were almost incapable of thinking for themselves.'

Lord Iron believes that Shriltasi is a place of evil, but the city Max discovers is merely different and he learns that magic can be used for the powers of good. His quest involves collecting the usual jewels, weapons and the other MacGuffins of fantasy literature, and the novel is typical sword and sorcery in that respect, although Moorcock and Constantine avoid presenting evil stereotypes.

The setting of the novel is not specifically representative of our own world, although there is a reference to the Egyptian goddess of fire, Sekmet, who has the head of a lioness and is linked with war and the sun. We are told that Karadur-Shriltasi is 'the core of the multiverse, that the fate of the city determines the nature of all ordered matter in myriad worlds and countless realities'. Humans, it seems, are the guardians of the multiverse, despite their many weaknesses and limitations. The weakness that particularly distinguishes humans is their natural prejudice and hostility to things and people who are different. Rose experiences a moment of enlightenment in which she sees the multiverse and her own relationship to it: 'All things were upon the web and if one strand vibrated, all others must feel it.' This is a valuable lesson — that actions do have consequences and effects on others.

Silverheart is an easy and exciting read, full of Gothic textures. It also contains a simple yet important message for its readers. As Max's own mother warns: 'It is a mistake to think that mundane reality is the only one.' It is for this very reason that everyone should read fantasy literature — to learn about the different truths and realities. Fantasy teaches us to dream, to expand our own knowledge and experience, and to look beyond our own limitations.

CODA

Moorcock's work is both avant-garde and popular. It has been translated into countless languages, yet his novels rarely reach the bestseller charts or even the university reading lists. Perhaps it is just that he is ahead of his time, or too experimental for the wider public, but his relative marginalisation might have something to do with the snobbery fantasy still inspires. There is also the problem of Moorcock's resistance to being pigeon-holed by any single genre. Although he is usually referred to as a science fiction writer by lazy booksellers and critics, he is not embraced by all SF or even all fantasy readers. This suits him well: Moorcock would rather be remembered as a popular author who broke the boundaries of conventional genres. The difficulty is that he falls between fantasy and mainstream literature.

Fantasy is an undervalued literary impulse. Since the Enlightenment, Western culture has placed more value on rational thinking and demanded a more exact form of naturalistic representation in its artistic expressions. Since then symbolism and myth have been regarded with some suspicion and, today, fantasy suffers from the same prejudice. It is important to remember that realism, like fantasy, is only another literary convention, as reality itself cannot be confined to materialistic description because it is full of ambiguity, dreams, paradox, symbol and mystery. Fantasy literature is surely a more accurate, if not satisfactory, form for expressing the complex reality of our own strange lives.

Fantasy has something important to offer in terms of re-evaluating our cultural heritage and offering insight into a more mystical and spiritual reality. Moorcock, as a writer, explores themes and subjects that others dare not confront. He is also an elusive and protean writer whose works blur the generic boundaries and is doing as much as anyone to bring fantasy into the literary mainstream.

What makes Moorcock's work stand above that of others, is that while some writers choose to present us with a microcosm of reality, Moorcock prefers the larger canvas of eternal time and space: not just this universe but the infinite continuum of the entire multiverse. Each myth he conjures challenges us in our own private struggles with chaos and order: 'I do celebrate the mythologising creativity of the human mind,' Moorcock wrote in 1998. 'As ecstatic dimension upon dimension unfolded, scattered, blended and bent, making every object a thing of intense beauty, sometimes of terror; as extraordinary encrusted patterns revealed themselves in the most familiar things, I was consumed with the most profound emotion at the harmony I sensed in the whole unseen multiverse.' [5]

Endnotes
1   Michael Moorcock in conversation with the author. See appendix: 'A Brief Interview with Michael Moorcock.'
2   All quotations that feature in the chapter headers are given by Michael Moorcock.
3   Notes taken by the author during 'An Evening with Michael Moorcock' at The Young Vic in London, 1993, where Moorcock was interviewed by Peter Ackroyd.
4   'A Child's Christmas in the Blitz,' *London Peculiar and Other Nonfiction*, PM Press, 2012.
5   Michael Moorcock, 'In the Know,' *Time Out*, 1998.

APPENDIX

Letter from Michael Moorcock

Dear Jeff:

Your questions gave me a lot of trouble. It's the old story, that you produce a metaphor — and if you could do it any other way, you wouldn't have produced the metaphor (i.e. something interpretable on any number of levels). My 'search' with the early Jerry Cornelius was for a method of telling a story which would allow for a pretty wide range of interpretation — in fact it was designed to be interpreted as the reader wished. Obviously, I have my own obsessions, but I tried to present a kind of actuality — symbolic, maybe, but very much in the terms and language of our present age, which I think began to be felt in the sixties and, indeed, predicted. It's not pleasant to have 'predicted' the Dubrovnik corpse boats, but the seeds of Balkan civil war were always there. You sensed it because nationalism was the only permissible alternative to communism and the rhetoric of nationalism is the only other rhetoric they're familiar with.

If *The Final Programme* was 'about' the dawning computer age, then *A Cure for Cancer* was my response to modern imperialism and Vietnam in particular, while, if you like, *The English Assassin* addressed the issues of Europe and British attitudes to them, while *The Condition of Muzak* acted as restatement, resolution and coda, and was structured internally that way as well. I'm very proud of the structuring of those novels, especially the last two. The first two were actually experimental, but the last two no longer were. I'd found that particular medium I needed. The reason I switched to a more conventional narrative in Pyat was because I'd discovered the one thing I hadn't really achieved in Cornelius was a sense of passing time. One's Mozart, the other's Wagner, as far as I'm concerned — and I make no comparisons of achievement, just of method! The short stories also, for me, have a certain assurance. Jerry is a technique. Another way of looking at it is to say Jerry is a response to the modern and I discovered modernist techniques to write it, as I did in *Mother London*. The Pyat novels, however, are a response to the modern in nineteenth century terms — i.e. pre-modern in choice of technique. I think of it as a Wagnerian method (i.e. late classicism) whereas Jerry is early modernism (Ives, perhaps, more than Schoenberg).

I think the zeitgeist threw up a number of people who weren't comfortable with the implications of the big bang theory. The idea that everything must ultimately dissipate. That's how I came up with the notion of the multiverse around the time that a few fringe theoretical physicists were doing the same thing. M-theory and Mandelbrot's ideas were very welcome to me since they gave a mathematical basis to ideas which I couldn't support scientifically. The notion of entropy was, for me, especially in my early years when I was full of teenage angst (and came up with Elric), to do with the inevitability of death. Being of an optimistic and, I hope, fairly realistic disposition, I decided that death might be inevitable but quality of life could be worked out in personal and social terms which would guarantee the best possible use of that span. Entropy has no moral quality, but it matters, in my view, how we deal with the fact.

The romantic tendency is to dramatise death, to give it a lot of Gothic luxury and rather avoid the fact (as in the current plague of vampire novels). As I said in *Wizardry and Wild Romance*, generic fantasy has a tendency to put on a good show, riding its richly-dressed war-horses up and down the ranks, but it's inclined to bolt at the first whiff of gunpowder. Jerry was an attempt to deal with the material of modern life without giving the reader much of an out. That's one reason for showing the 'real' Jerry as a bit of a wanker, an obvious failure, while his mother always acts as a chorus, in case we should forget… I tended to want anyone who was identifying with Jerry to be caught up short by the final volume. Chaos tends to diffusion and Law tends to stagnation. Preserving something can kill it as successfully as letting it disintegrate.

Moderation in all things… This is my somewhat conventional belief — a sort of Epicureanism — that life should be enjoyed to the full and that its responsibilities should be taken seriously.

I was attracted to aestheticism as a lad — I was far too robust to be able to emulate any of my pallid heroes, except possibly Richard Le Gallienne, and he was far too robust to be a hero. I read Pater and Ruskin and Whistler and all that. Greenery-yallery, blue and white. I longed to look pale but interesting. Anyway, those ideas are very attractive to me — epicurianism, I mean. But I was anxious to avoid traditional versions. I was and still am very interested in popular fiction as a form and was to a large degree looking for new popular forms, much as Hart or Hammerstein or Sondheim (or even Weill) did. I think there comes a point where you can hardly help writing 'literary' fiction, but that's another story.

I wrote *The Sundered Worlds* in 1960-61. In it I had a character who could sense the rest of the unseen multiverse and who in the end does come to see it in all its infinite glory — a populated space rather than the vacuum proposed by others. I also abhor a vacuum and so filled up the multiverse with millions of previously unseen worlds. Later, I had people with the same sensibilities simply walk between one universe and the other. Incidentally, there's a slightly more sophisticated version of SW in *The Coming of the Terraphiles*, the Dr Who novel I did a year or two back. It's actually a better version of SW but using many of the same themes. It also allows for dark matter etc. Although I had a sort of black hole in SW I hadn't of course named it. Science, in my view, is no less free of reflecting humanity's deep emotional desires than anything else we use to examine our environment and our place in it.

God is probably the Cosmic Balance... My understanding of all this stuff has become refined through the fiction, so it's very hard to say what my 'intentions' were in the earlier work, since I hardly knew them myself. I've played different riffs on the ideas. If anything, the hermaphrodite in *The Final Programme* (&c) is a failed ideal, a little bit of a disappointment, but not altogether unsuccessful. I'm thinking about God and who created whom quite a bit in my current partly autobiographical fantasy, *The Whispering Swarm*. I rather enjoy not knowing — none of us can ever know — which came first. Even if we have a perpetually self-renewing multiverse, as I have in my cosmology, we still don't know where it all started. Good to speculate about, though.

The changes in the penultimate chapter of *Gloriana* are relatively minor, so as not to disturb anything else in the book. They're easily compared. They were written in response to several women arguing that this scene, as it was written, could be seen as a justification of rape. Gloriana's failure to achieve orgasm was to do with her repression, her having to fulfil her function as a symbol. In that there's some thematic similarity between *Gloriana* and *Behold the Man*. By asserting her own identity, her own needs, she also breaks free of the terrible burden of being a living symbol. I saw most women as living with that kind of burden. I was trying, if this doesn't sound too nuts, to 'reverse' the idealising allegory of *The Fairy Queen* and give Gloriana back her humanity.

I'm also very fond of Quire. I would say that love, in the form I most admired it, was a respect for, and celebration of, the individuality of others, a positive desire to understand and enjoy the world. It's not a sentimental notion and has almost nothing to do with romantic love in its later versions. A third novel can be mentioned here — a minor one done either as *Constant Fire* or *The Transformation of Miss Mavis Ming* — in which Mavis finds fulfilment in the Fireclown's attack on her body. This struck me as a misguided notion. I realised, from personal experience, that this kind of fulfilment is essentially empty emotional calories and neither lasts nor achieves very much positive. *The Brothel in Rosenstrasse* is in some ways a re-examination of the ideas in the original *Constant Fire* and *Gloriana*.

The Eternal Champion was first drafted when I was seventeen. The novella was written when I was twenty-one or twenty-two. I had an inclination to self-dramatisation in those days. The exorcism of that aspect of myself probably came first with *Behold the Man* and later with *Breakfast in the Ruins*. I really do think that if we make an effort to 'love one another' we could produce a pretty good quality of life all round. On the other hand, as someone active in politics, I know how hard that can be to achieve without the group-will driving the desire. We're an easily distracted bunch of monkeys. So I'm trying to deal realistically, if you like, with very romantic ideas. That's also a theme in *The Whispering Swarm*, my current work in progress.

I think some aspects of The Eternal Champion are as you describe, but many, such as in Corum and Hawkmoon, are fundamentally humanistic — we can change if we get rid of 'gods'. I have a belief in the randomness of the natural world, but I do not believe in 'fate'. I am involved in politics. That means I believe it's possible to change the human condition for the better (or the worse) — I'm just not sure to what degree. Sometimes I wonder if it's worth it, but it's in my nature to be optimistic and try to work for things to improve. That relates, for instance, to my championship of the women's movement and my admiration for Andrea Dworkin.

Things could be a great deal better in the West, let alone the rest of the world, and the means of making them better are within our power. What disgusts me is the self-centred, self-important people who refuse to consider those means — mostly powerful white men with a vested interest in social disharmony. We are still driven by the compunctions of the beast which helped us survive but which are now pretty much anti-survival. I still try to find a balance between the beast in me and the man in me. Controlling our inner beast might be a worthwhile goal.

How do I keep so disciplined? Well, it's not quite so simple when you're at my end of things. But, put simply, it's my job. It's been my source of income since I was sixteen. I hardly know any other way of working. The piece in *London Peculiar* and *Into the Media Web* (my published collections of non-fiction) pretty accurately describes what I go through. In general I find it harder to write than I once did, because my ambitions grow. I have to find ways of telling a story so that it can't be confused with readers' expectations about the way a story 'should' develop. Ultimately this means more thinking in the modernist terms I tended to reject. It rarely gets any easier. I have enormous anxieties, at least until I'm ready to start work in earnest. I still find it very hard to identify those anxieties for what they are.

That said, I have a facility. I can still write a novel in less than a month *(Revenge of the Rose,* for instance) and get a considerable pleasure from the actual processes of structuring something (assuming I've achieved what I hoped to achieve, which isn't always), whereas I've learned that most people have a hard time learning those principles — it's a gift for structure which in the main creates prolific composers, playwrights, novelists and even painters; an instinct examined and refined, if you like.

I was expelled from my school partly because I kept the other kids awake every night telling stories (mostly pinched from the likes of Kipling). I enjoy the business of telling a story. I have developed ways of harnessing and channelling those anxieties to power the work itself. I grew up in a school of journalism where frequently the deadlines were a matter of a few hours, let alone days or weeks. That teaches you to write 800 words concisely and vividly. 1,500 words is a luxury. That's why I still do a fair bit of newspaper journalism. It reminds me to be concise.

They say that computers make you lazy and too windy. This could be true. Another good training is writing comics. I wrote a lot of comic strips in my early career, which few people have a facility for doing, and this taught me (see *Death is No Obstacle!*) to cut out a lot of fat — narrative, picture, dialogue — and keep the story moving forward. This training gives you a large repertoire of short cuts which you have to unlearn if you want to write a certain kind of fiction.

I helped create the foundations of modern romantic fantasy but those techniques and style, even, can become obstacles if you're trying to tell a story of character. Much of the seventies was spent by me in unlearning what I'd actually taught a lot of the writers who followed me. I find that that happens fairly often. Once a technique or a notion is absorbed into the common genre I no longer find it very useful. For some reason I think good fiction like good rock'n'roll should have elements of risk in it.

You should begin a new book as if you have never read one. The reader should feel the author's uncertainty even while they accept the author's authority. Does that make sense?

All best
Michael Moorcock
2012

A Brief Interview with Michael Moorcock

JEFF GARDNER: *How influential was the war to your writing?*
MICHAEL MOORCOCK: Wartime London had an enormous effect on my imagination. It is a very peculiar landscape. It's a malleable landscape — wasteland and ruins as you grow up. Your entire memory is one of something in transition: something between being one thing and another. So that kind of landscape, I think, probably is the single greatest effect on my writing.

How did your schooling affect your outlook on life?
I had a strong influence in Rudolf Steiner when I was a small child and I think it stuck with me for some time in many ways and I don't mind it having stuck. Steiner was interested in 'mystical cosmology' and moral action; his whole philosophy was very gentle and, as it were, kind. I was always attracted to the ideas of cosmic consciousness even if never interested in practising it. I got most of my basic ideas from Steiner as well as from writers of the fifties like Poul Anderson and Fritz Lieber.

What are your hobbies?
Work, travelling, walking, climbing. I also collect ephemera. I've done my stint of haymaking.

What do you enjoy reading?
So many writers. I was reading everything from an early age. George Bernard Shaw, Dickens, Nesbit, ER Burroughs, EJ Henty, Haggard — good adventure story writers. Also George Eliot and more obscure writers like Adam Smith. Peake was my strong inspiration. I have a wide range of tastes

Have you ever used drugs to stimulate your writing?
I do believe hallucinatory drugs can aid creativity but, oddly enough, I rarely use them in that respect. I had a reputation for writing everything on acid, which is simply completely untrue. I am very prone to visions, of seeing things that are not there, or inventing things out of what is there — a very intense visual imagination. Therefore, I'm doing a lot of the same things as people who have dropped acid and the intensity gives my work that quality. Drugs are not to be given to anyone under forty. You have to be mature and responsible.

What is your opinion of science fiction?
I don't really have any great talent for writing SF. My imagination doesn't lead in that direction. SF demands a kind of rationalism, a kind of reductionism, which does rationalise the imagination in a way I find uncomfortable. Fantasy is more flexible.

How would you define fantasy?
I don't believe there is such a thing as fantasy or science fiction or detective fiction and so on. I think there are certain writers who in their field shine and in every one of those fields you'll get some good writers emerging. Sometimes the field itself can limit the writer's work and then frequently the writer does something about it. I hate generic terms.

Why do you think Elric is so popular?
I have a feeling people like ambiguous characters — they have to interpret them. I think Elric and Dracula have certain things in common — vulnerability as well as a penchant for violence. That seems to be the formula people like. It was not ever conceived cynically.

Explain your use of entropy.

We use up a lot of energy, collapse and grow cold. I believe in a sense, human love conquers entropy and that you'll find running through a lot of my books.

Is the Pyat in 'Between the Wars' the same as the character in the Jerry Cornelius books?

There's a malleability about all those people that means they can never be quite exactly the same characters in any given story. So I wouldn't say he was exactly the same, but I think of him as being the same. I think of him as the same character in different circumstances. Mostly what you find with my characters is that the characters stay the same but their circumstances change. When circumstances change they frequently act differently, behave differently, say something differently or their attitude is different. We are all something else in altered circumstances.

Hawkwind: Michael Moorcock & Robert Calvert

Psychedelic prog rock band Hawkwind explore science fiction themes that appeal to their drug fuelled trips into 'inner space'. As lyricist/singer Robert Calvert became increasingly unstable Moorcock took to standing in for him, contributing his own poems and lyrics. By his own admission, Moorcock is no poet, but his song lyrics are playful and vivid. His dramatic poem 'Sonic Attack' is still performed at concerts — most famously on the *Space Ritual* tour and live album:

> *These are the first signs of Sonic Attack:*
> *You will notice small objects, such as ornaments, oscillating.*
> *You will notice a vibration in your diaphragm.*
> *You will hear a distant hissing in your ears.*
> *You will feel dizzy.*
> *You will feel the need to vomit.*
> *There will be bleeding from orifices.*
> *There will be an ache in the pelvic region.*
> *You may be subject to fits of hysterical shouting,*
> *or even laughter.*

It is a histrionic and slightly manic message from a faceless authority whose words become a parody of government information leaflets which claim to protect its citizens from nuclear war. The words also humorously exaggerate the effects of any great rock concert.

On the 1975 album, *Warrior on the Edge of Time*, Moorcock provided three poems, performing two of them himself, as well as lyrics for the song 'Kings of Speed'. Lyrically, the best is 'Warriors', with its elegant use of metaphor and repetition:

> *We are humanity's scythe to sweep this way and that*
> *And cut the enemy down as weeds*
> *We are humanity's spade to dig up the roots*
> *Wherever they have grown*
> *We are humanity's fire to burn the waste to the finest ash*
> *We are wind which will blow the ash away*
> *As if it had never existed.*

'The Wizard Blew his Horn' fits in well with the Eternal Champion mythos — especially the Erekosë series:

> *The great hound barked and the world turned white*
> *The great hound sighed and the forest died*
> *The wizard blew his horn*
>
> *The eagle laughed and the world grew black*
> *It stretched giant claws and it snatched the Law*
> *And the champion stirred in his sleep*

Moorcock does not always take himself seriously and much of his work contains satire and humour. Hawkwind's 1982 album *Choose Your Masques* included two songs by Moorcock; the title track and 'Arrival In Utopia':

> *We dreamed of steel and glass and wire*
> *Of days of wine and nights of fire*
> *We dreamt of dogs that talked like boys*
> *Of girls who flew, of unnamed joys.*

And now our dreams are true
We don't know what to do
'Cause we don't like it here
There's nothing for us to fear
Bored mindless in utopia.

In 1985 Hawkwind released *The Chronicle of the Black Sword*, which follows the exploits of Moorcock's famous fantasy hero, Elric. The Moorcock penned song, 'Sleep Of A Thousand Tears', has both evocative lyrics and a great guitar solo. It is a song of love, quest and heroism. Opening with the tender image, 'With your white arms wrapped around me,' two lovers awake in a dream-world:

And the landscape boiled
With a million strange flowers
And a sun set in the East

The song then drifts into a romantic and never-ending journey, as it segues into a sublime guitar solo:

And we rode to a land at the edge of the skies
To an emerald tower on a hill.

Hawkwind's other writer in residence was Robert Calvert, SF poet and novelist who also contributed to sixties underground magazine, *Frendz*. Calvert has developed something of a cult following and his writing is of an imaginative and literary quality with a unique blend of metaphor, wordplay and surrealism. Calvert's lyrics for 'Spirit of the Age' (1977) demonstrate his irony and wit:

I would've liked you to have been deep frozen too
And waiting still as fresh in your flesh for my return to earth
But your father refused to sign the forms to freeze you...
Your android replica is playing up again, but it's no joke
When she comes she moans another's name.

In a different tone, Calvert's 'Damnation Alley' (1977) is based on the Roger Zelazny post-nuclear holocaust novel of the same name and is written using extremely effective rhyme and rhythm that reflects the urgent mood of escape.

Ride the post-atomic radioactive trash
The sky's on fire from that nuclear flash
Diving through the burning hoop of doom
In an eight wheeled anti-radiation tomb.

Calvert's use of metaphor is always vivid and original. For example, in 'High Rise' (1977), the skyscraper is described as 'a flypaper stuck with human life' and when someone is pushed from a window his body on the pavement becomes a 'Starfish of human blood shape / Tentacles of human gore'. Calvert's most psychedelic lyrics are contained in the song 'Steppenwolf' (1976), inspired by Herman Hesse's masterly novel about madness and altered states of mind, in which Calvert evokes a strange mood of melancholy and paranoia through his use of certain abstract images to reflect the changing emotions of the despairing voice of the narrator. Note also the subtle use of alliteration.

The moon's a howling mouth of mercury
Quicksilver quivering in the sky
It echoes like a cave of chromium
They'll vacuum up my soul when I die.

In the same song, and typical of Calvert's style, he chooses precise vocabulary to metaphorically describe the eyes of the man-wolf: 'My eyes are convex lenses of ebony / Embedded in amber.'

Calvert was an artist using words to paint portraits of urban and futuristic fantasy and his death in 1988 was tragic and untimely. He certainly was a visionary — but whether this was inspired by genius or acid is left purely to conjecture.

A Michael Moorcock Miscellany

Here follows a list of Michael Moorcock's novels, short story collections, non-fiction and many of the comics and graphic novels, although trying to bring order to the chaos is a complicated procedure as Moorcock has produced something close to 100 books. I also touch on his involvement with music.

Not all of Moorcock's books are still in print and sometimes titles have been changed. Many short stories have been collected in different anthologies a number of times.

Beginning in 1992, British publishers Millennium/Orion reissued practically all the titles that fit into his *Eternal Champion Multiverse* in fourteen weighty volumes, of which the largest exceeds 800 pages. This was done with the help of John Davey. The series attempts to create a uniform omnibus collection of these particular books and involves some revision. Most of the amendments are slight, involving names, so that familiar characters can be reincarnated to make interconnections more explicit.

For a more complete bibliography please see John Davey's *Michael Moorcock: A Reader's Guide* (Jayde Design) or The Tanelorn Archives. There are also a number of excellent bibliographies online.

ELRIC
This listing is complicated by the fact that many of the Elric stories appear in different editions and under different titles.
The Stealer of Souls (Neville Spearman 1963)
Stormbringer (Herbert Jenkin s1965)
The Singing Citadel (Mayflower 1970)
The Sleeping Sorceress (NEL 1971) aka *The Vanishing Tower*
    (Daw 1977)

THE LAW OF CHAOS

Elric of Melniboné (Hutchinson 1972)
The Jade Man's Eyes (Unicorn 1973)
The Sailor on the Seas of Fate (Quartet 1976)
The Weird of the White Wolf (Daw 1977)
The Bane of the Black Sword (NEL 1977)
The Fortress of the Pearl (Gollancz 1989)
The Revenge of the Rose (Grafton 1991)

EREKOSË
The Eternal Champion (Dell 1970: novella 1962)
Phoenix In Obsidian (Mayflower 1970)
The Swords of Heaven, The Flowers of Hell (Star 1979)
The Dragon In the Sword (Ace 1986)

HAWKMOON
The Jewel In the Skull (Lancer 1967)
The Mad God's Amulet (Lancer 1968)
The Sword Of the Dawn (Lancer 1968)
The Runestaff (Mayflower 1969)
Count Brass (Mayflower 1973).
The Champion of Garathorm (Mayflower 1973)
The Quest for Tanelorn (Mayflower 1975)

CORUM
The Knight of the Swords (Berkley 1971)
The Queen of the Swords (Berkley 1971)
The King of the Swords (Berkley 1971)
The Bull and the Spear (Allison & Busby 1973)
The Oak and the Ram (Allison & Busby 1973)
The Sword and the Stallion (Allison & Busby 1974)

WARRIOR OF MARS
City of the Beast aka *Warriors of Mars* (Compact 1965)
Lord of the Spiders aka *Blades of Mars* (Compact 1965)
Master of the Pit aka *Barbarians of Mars* (Compact 1965)

JERRY CORNELIUS
The Final Programme (Avon 1968)
A Cure For Cancer (Allison & Busby 1971)
The English Assassin (Allison & Busby 1972)
The Condition of Muzak (Allison & Busby 1977)
The Adventures of Una Persson & Catherine Cornelius in the Twentieth Century (Quartet 1976)
The Lives and Times of Jerry Cornelius (Allison & Busby 1976)
The Great Rock'n'Roll Swindle aka *Gold Diggers of 1977* (Virgin 1980)
The Entropy Tango (NEL 1981)
The Opium General and Other Stories (Harrap 1984)
The Nature of the Catastrophe (Savoy 1971) stories by MM et al
Firing the Cathedral (PS Publishing 2002)

NOMAD OF THE TIME STREAMS
The Warlord of the Air (Ace 1971)
The Land Leviathan (Quartet 1974)
The Steel Tsar (Granada 1981)

THE DANCERS AT THE END OF TIME
An Alien Heat (MacGibbon & Kee 1972)
The Hollow Lands (Harper & Row 1974)
The End of All Songs (Harper & Row 1976)
Legends from the End of Time (WH Allen 1976)
The Transformation of Miss Mavis Ming (WH Allen 1977)
Elric At the End of Time (Paper Tiger 1981)

THE LAW OF CHAOS

GLOGAUER
Behold the Man (Allison & Busby 1969)
Breakfast In the Ruins (NEL 1972)

VON BEK
The War Hound and the World's Pain (Granada 1981)
The Brothel in Rosenstrasse (NEL 1982)
The City in the Autumn Stars (Grafton 1986)
The Dreamthief's Daughter (Earthlight 2001)
The Skrayling Tree (Earthlight 2002)
The White Wolf's Son (Warner 2005)

BETWEEN THE WARS
Byzantium Endures (Secker and Warburg 1981)
The Laughter of Carthage (Secker and Warburg 1984)
Jerusalem Commands (Jonathan Cape 1992)
The Vengeance of Rome (Jonathan Cape 2006)

THE SECOND ETHER
Blood (Millennium 1994)
Fabulous Harbours (Millennium1995)
The War Amongst the Angels (Orion 1996)

NOVELS
The Winds of Limbo aka *The Fireclown* (Compact 1965)
The Blood Red Game aka *The Sundered Worlds* (Compact 1965)
The Shores of Death aka *The Twilight Man* (Compact 1966)
Somewhere In The Night (Compact 1966) aka *The Chinese Agent*
The Printer's Devil (Compact 1966) aka *The Russian Intelligence*
The Wrecks of Time (Ace 1967) aka *The Rituals of Infinity*
    (Arrow 1971)
The Ice Schooner (1969)

The Black Corridor (1969) with Hilary Bailey
The Distant Suns (1975) with James Cawthorn
Gloriana; or, The Unfulfill'd Queen (Allison and Busby 1978; revised Phoenix 1993)
The Golden Barge (Savoy 1979) written in 1957
Mother London (Secker and Warburg 1988)
The King of the City (Scribner 2000)
Silverheart (Earthlight 2000) with Storm Constantine
Doctor Who: The Coming of the Terraphiles (BBC Books 2010)

COLLECTIONS
The Time Dweller (Rupert Hart-Davis 1969)
Moorcock's Book of Martyrs (Quartet 1976)
Sojan (Savoy 1977)
My Experiences in the Third World War (Savoy 1980)
Casablanca (Victor Gollancz 1989)
Tales From the Texas Woods (Mojo 1997)
London Bone (Scribner 2001)
Modem Times 2.0 (PM Press 2011)

NON-FICTION
The Retreat From Liberty (Zomba Books 1983)
Letters From Hollywood (Harrap 1986) art by Michael Foreman
Wizardry and Wild Romance (V. Gollancz 1987)
Fantasy: The 100 Best Books (Xanadu 1988) with James Cawthorn
Death Is No Obstacle (Savoy 1992) interviews with Colin Greenland
Into the Media Web: Selected Short Nonfiction 1956-2006 (Savoy Books 2010)
London Peculiar and Other Nonfiction (PM Press 2012)

ILLUSTRATED BOOKS
Elric: The Return to Melnibone (Jayde Design 1997) illustrated
  by Druillet
The Sunday Books (Duckworth Overlook 2011) illustrated by
  Mervyn Peake

AS EDITOR
Tarzan Adventures (1957-58)
Sexton Blake Library (1959-61)
New Worlds no. 142-207 (1964 to 1973)
  and no. 212-216 (1978-79) & no. 221 (1996)
SF Reprise (1966-67)

MUSIC
Deep Fix: *New World's Fair* (UAG 1975: Griffen CD 1995)
Deep Fix: *Brothel In Rosenstrasse* (Cyborg 1992)
Hawkwind: *Warrior On the Edge of Time* (UAG 1975)
Hawkwind: *Sonic Attack* (RCA 1981)
Hawkwind: *Choose Your Masques* (RCA 1982)
Hawkwind: *Zones* (Flicknife 1983)
Hawkwind: *Live Chronicles* (Griffen 1994)
Moorcock has also worked with:
  Brian Eno
  Robert Calvert (on the albums *Hype* and *Lucky Leif*)
  Nik Turner
  Blue Öyster Cult (for whom he wrote the songs 'Black Blade',
  'Veteran Of The Psychic Wars' and 'The Great Sun Jester')
Singer on Spirits Burning CD *Alien Injection* (2008), tracks
  'Entropy Tango' & 'Gloriana'

COMICS
Moorcock wrote innumerable comic strips for Fleetway and

Amalgamated Press in the 1960s, including adventures with Kit Carson, Billy the Kid and Dogfight Dixon.

The Adventures of Jerry Cornelius comic strip appeared in *International Times* no. 57-71, and a Hawkwind related strip appeared in *Frendz* no. 16. Elric related stories have also appeared in *Conan the Barbarian* comics (Marvel Comics 1972) no. 14-15.

Michael Moorcock's Multiverse (DC 1998) no. 1-12 with Walter Simonson

Elric: the Making of a Sorcerer (DC 2004-6) no. 1-4 with Walter Simonson

GRAPHIC NOVELS (adaptations of Moorcock's work)
The Swords of Heaven, The Flowers of Hell (Simon & Schuster 1979)
The Dreaming City (Epic 1980)
The Jewel In the Skull (Savoy 1986) James Cawthorn
The Crystal and the Amulet (Savoy 1986) James Cawthorn
Stormbringer (Savoy) James Cawthorn
Elric of Melniboné (First Comics 1987) Thomas & Russell
Elric: Sailor on the Seas of Fate (First Comics 1987) written by Roy Thomas, artwork by Michael T Gilbert & George Freeman
Corum (First Comics 1987) by Mike Mignola & Mike Baron
Stormbringer (Dark Horse/Topps 1998) P Craig Russell
Elric: The Balance Lost (Boom Studios 2012) Roberson & Biagini

FILM
The Land that Time Forgot (dir: Kevin Connor 1975) screenplay co-written with James Cawthorn based on the novel by ER Burroughs

SOURCES

WEBSITES
www.multiverse.org — Moorcock's Miscellany: the official
    Moorcock Site
www.novymir.com.au/terminalcafe/analysis.html
www.eclipse.co.uk/sweetdespise/moorcock

SELECT BIBLIOGRAPHY
Aldiss, Brian *The Trillion Year Spree* (Victor Gollancz 1986)
Arnheim, Rudolf *Entropy and Art* (California 1971)
Bakhtin, Mikhail *Rabelais and His World* (Indiana 1984)
Ballard, JG *A User's Guide to the Millennium* (Flamingo 1997)
Bradbury, Malcolm *The Modern British Novel* (Penguin 1993)
Burns & Sugnet *The Imagination on Trial* (Allison & Busby 1981)
Camp, L Sprague de *Literary Swordsmen & Sorcerers*
    (Wisconsin 1976)
Caracciolo, Peter *The Arabian Nights in English Literature*
    (MacMillan 1988)
Carter, Angela *Expletives Deleted* (Chatto & Windus 1992)
Clute, J & John Grant *The Encyclopedia of Fantasy* (Orbit 1997)
Cupitt, Don *The Sea of Faith* (BBC Books 1984)
Foucault, Michael *Politics, Philosophy, Culture* (London 1988)
Frazer, James *The Golden Bough* (MacMillan 1923)
Freud, Sigmund *The Interpretation of Dreams* (Penguin 1991)
Gleick, James *Chaos* (Abacus 1987)
Greenland, Colin *The Entropy Exhibition* (Routledge, Kegan &
    Paul 1983)
Hebdige, Dick *Subculture* (Methuen 1970)
Jung, CG *Modern Man In Search of a Soul* (Routledge 1933)
Kropotkin, Peter *The Conquest of Bread* (Cambridge 1995)

Manlowe, CN *Science Fiction: Ten Explorations* (Ohio 1986)

Melly, George *Revolt Into Style* (Oxford 1970)

Nicholls, Stan *Wordsmiths of Wonder* (Orbit 1993)

Nietzsche, Friedrich *The Birth of Tragedy* (Penguin 1993)

Nuttall, Jeff *Bomb Culture* (MacGibbon & Kee 1968)

Platt, Charles *Dream Makers* (Xanadu 1980)

Punter, David *The Literature of Terror* Vol 1 & Vol 2
    (Longman 1996)

Raban, Jonathan *Soft City* (Hamilton 1974)

Rabkin, Eric *The Fantastic in Literature* (Princeton 1976)

Savage, Jon *England's Dreaming* (Faber 1991)

Scholes, Robert *Fabulation and Metafiction* (Illinois 1979)

Scholes & Rabkin *Science Fiction: Histroy, Science, Vision*
    (Oxford 1977)

Schweitzer, D (ed) *Exploring Fantasy Worlds* (Borgo Press 1985)

Steiner, Rudolf *The Philosophy of Freedom* (Steiner Press 1916)

Tawn, Brian *Dude's Dreams: the Music of Michael Moorcock*
    (Hawkfan Publications 1997)

ABOUT THE AUTHOR

Jeff Gardiner lives in the UK and is the author of three novels: *Myopia*, *Igboland* and *Treading On Dreams*. His short story collection, *A Glimpse of the Numinous*, contains horror, slipstream fiction and humour. Many of his stories are available in anthologies and magazines, and he has had articles translated into German.

For more information please go to <www.jeffgardiner.com> and <www.jeffgardiner.wordpress.com>

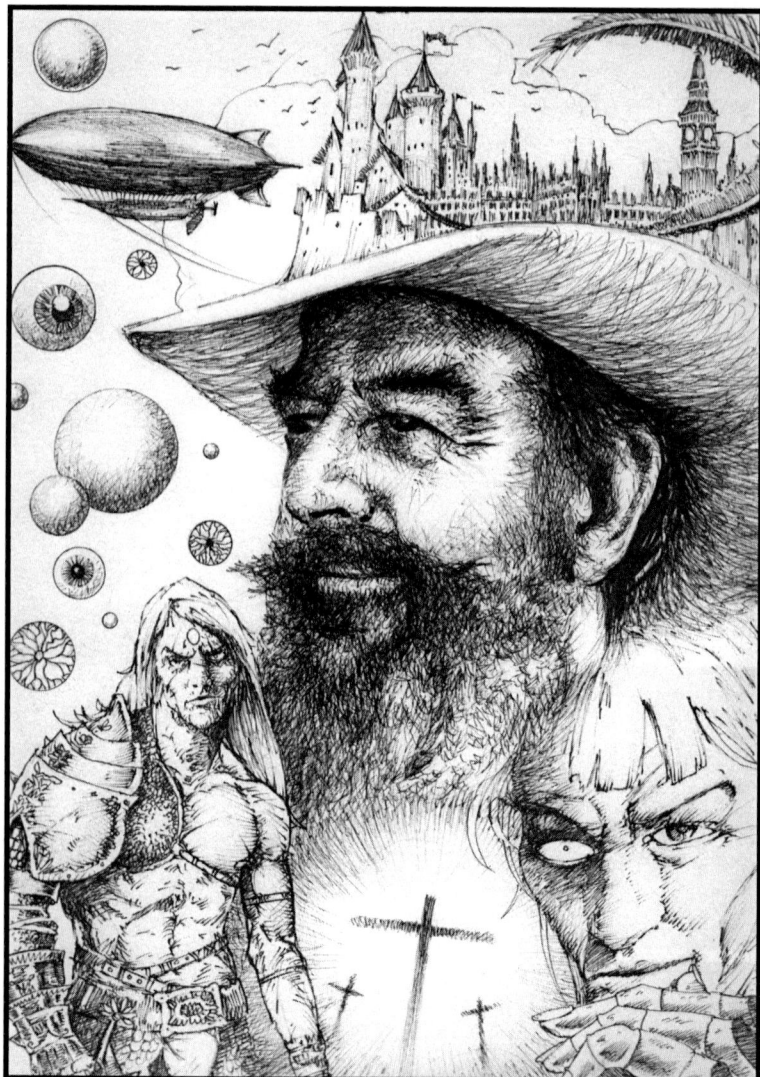

Illus. This page: Bob Covington
Next page, bottom right & title page: Malcolm Laverty

COVER GALLERY

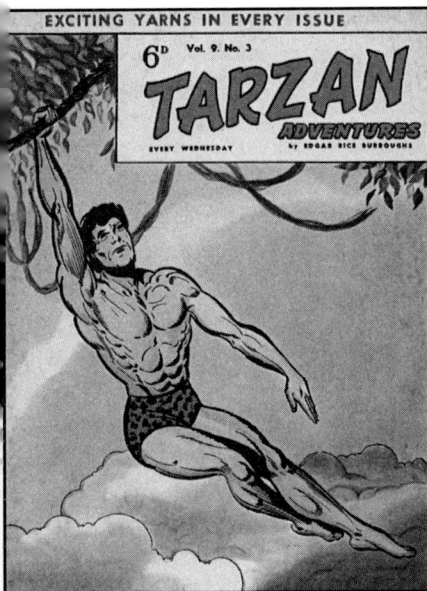

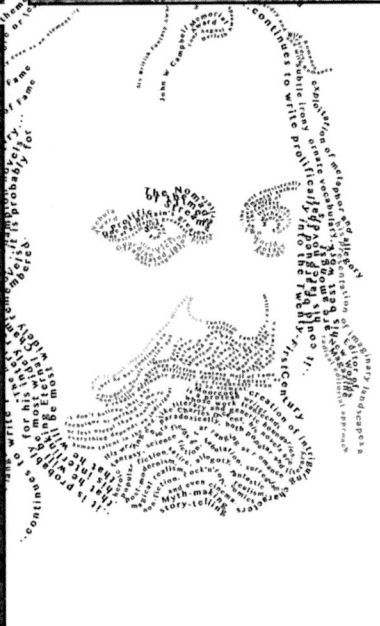

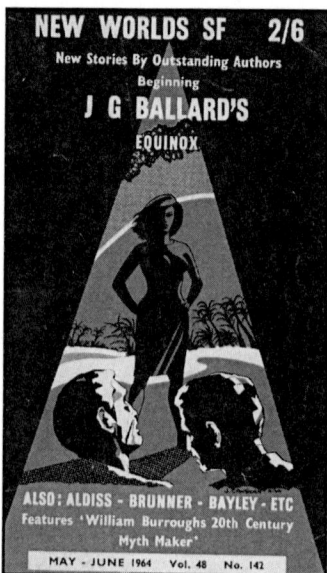

New Worlds SF cover — NEW WORLDS SF 2/6. New Stories By Outstanding Authors. Beginning J G BALLARD'S EQUINOX. ALSO: ALDISS - BRUNNER - BAYLEY - ETC. Features 'William Burroughs 20th Century Myth Maker'. MAY - JUNE 1964 Vol. 48 No. 142

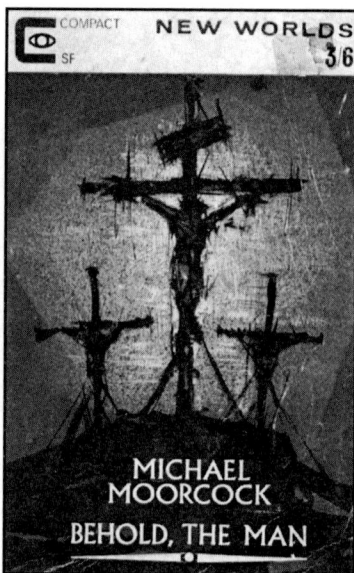

New Worlds cover — COMPACT SF. NEW WORLDS 3/6. MICHAEL MOORCOCK. BEHOLD, THE MAN

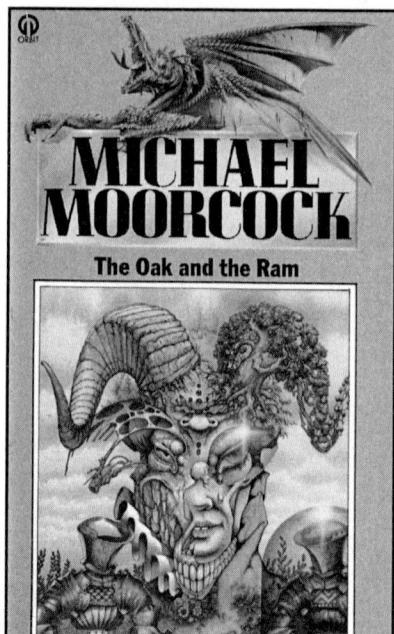

MICHAEL MOORCOCK — The Oak and the Ram

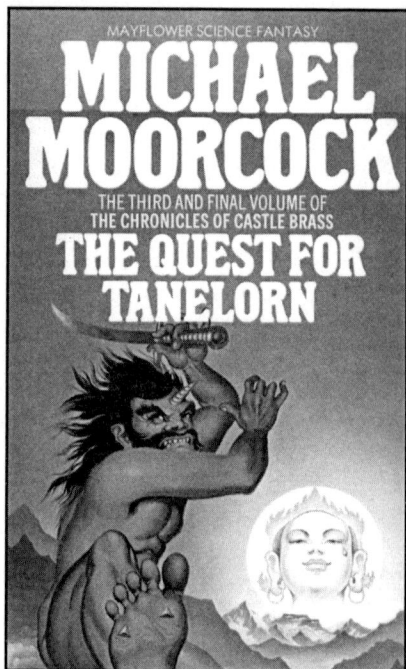

MAYFLOWER SCIENCE FANTASY. MICHAEL MOORCOCK. THE THIRD AND FINAL VOLUME OF THE CHRONICLES OF CASTLE BRASS. THE QUEST FOR TANELORN

Science Fantasy

No. 47
VOLUME 16
2/6

The Dreaming City

by MICHAEL MOORCOCK

MAYFLOWER SCIENCE FANTASY

MOORCOCK
The Final Programme

The final novel of the
Jerry Cornelius quartet

'One of the most ambitious, illuminating and
enjoyable works of fiction published in English
since the war' Angus Wilson, *Observer*

MICHAEL MOORCOCK
The Condition Of Muzak

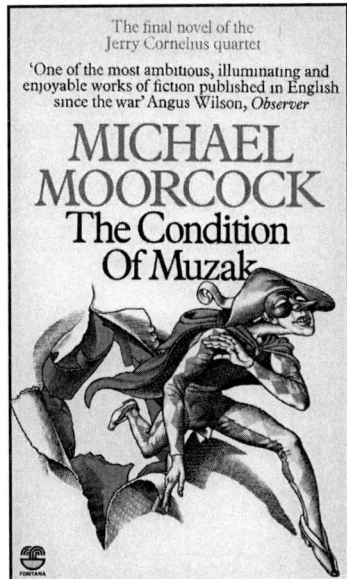

FONTANA

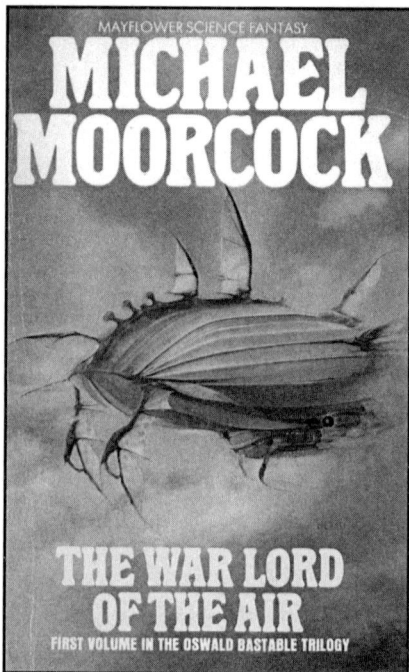

MICHAEL MOORCOCK

THE WAR LORD OF THE AIR

FIRST VOLUME IN THE OSWALD BASTABLE TRILOGY

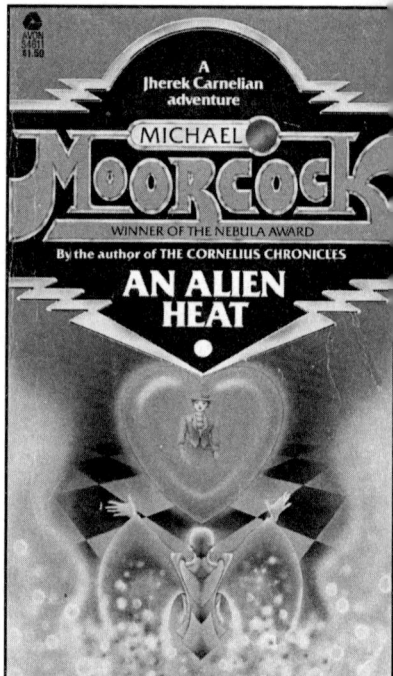

A Jherek Carnelian adventure

MICHAEL MOORCOCK

WINNER OF THE NEBULA AWARD

By the author of THE CORNELIUS CHRONICLES

AN ALIEN HEAT

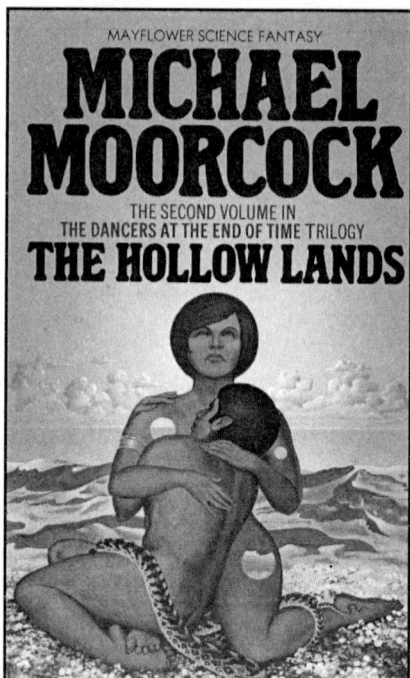

MICHAEL MOORCOCK

THE SECOND VOLUME IN
THE DANCERS AT THE END OF TIME TRILOGY

THE HOLLOW LANDS

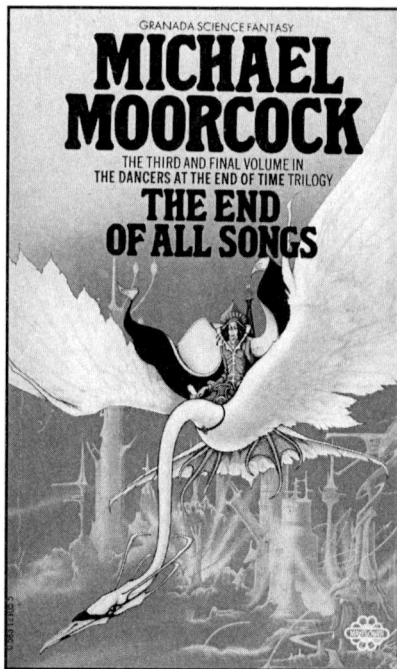

MICHAEL MOORCOCK

THE THIRD AND FINAL VOLUME IN
THE DANCERS AT THE END OF TIME TRILOGY

THE END OF ALL SONGS

GLORIANA
OR
THE UNFULFILL'D QUEEN

BEING A ROMANCE BY
MICHAEL
MOORCOCK

Published in the year ANNO DOMINI MCMLXXVIII by
FONTANA PAPERBACKS
LONDON

'The best fantasy novel of the year.'
Isaac Asimov's Science Fiction Magazine

MICHAEL MOORCOCK
The War Hound
and the
World's Pain

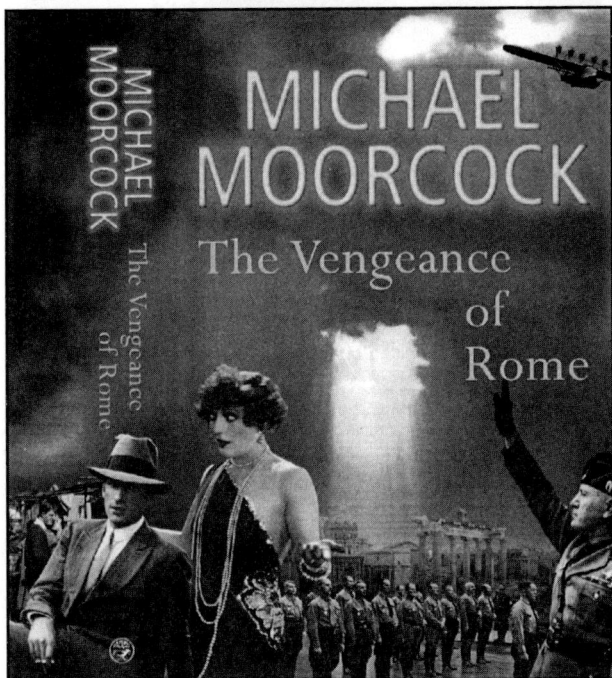

MICHAEL
MOORCOCK

MICHAEL
MOORCOCK

The Vengeance
of Rome

The Vengeance
of Rome

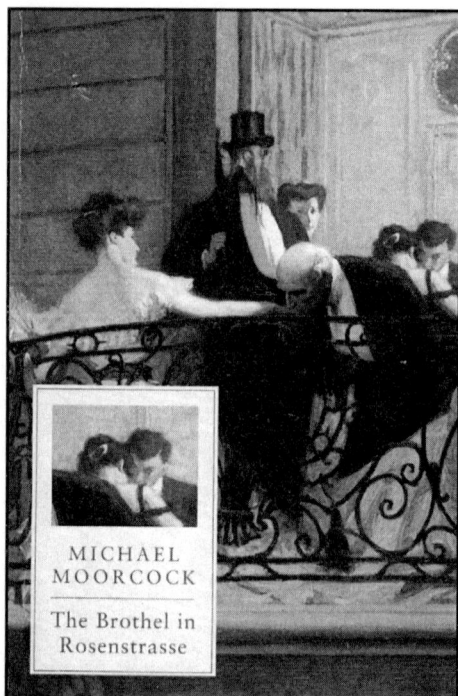

MICHAEL
MOORCOCK

The Brothel in
Rosenstrasse

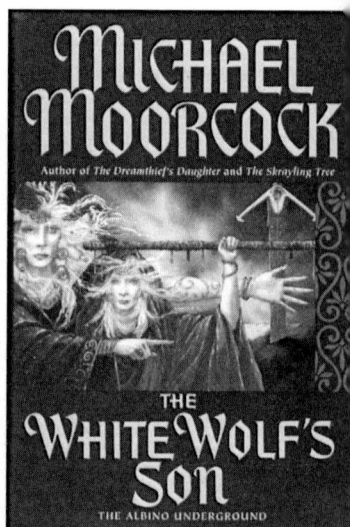

MICHAEL
MOORCOCK

Author of *The Dreamthief's Daughter* and *The Skrayling Tree*

THE
WHITE WOLF'S
SON

THE ALBINO UNDERGROUND

THE CHRONICLE OF THE
BLACK SWORD

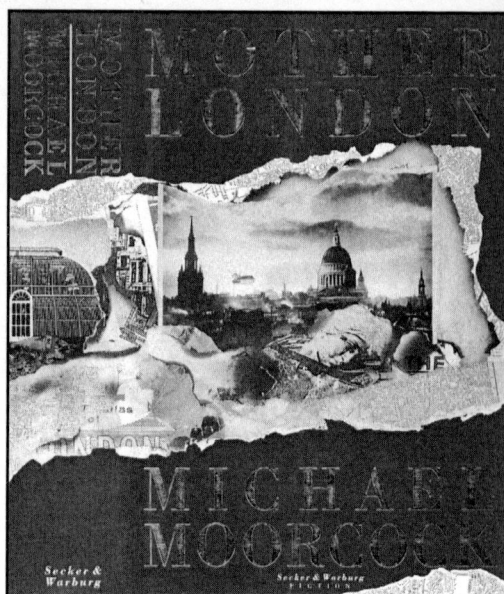

MOTHER
LONDON

MICHAEL
MOORCOCK

Secker &
Warburg

Secker & Warburg
FICTION

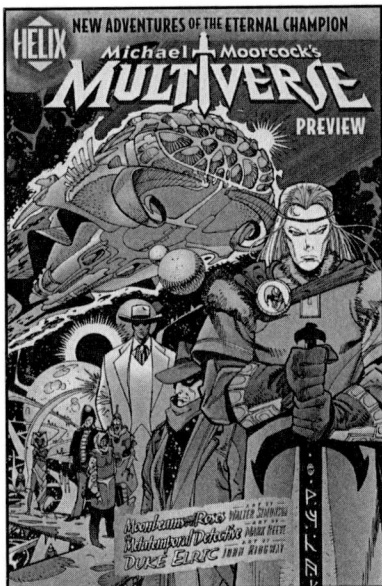

NEW ADVENTURES OF THE ETERNAL CHAMPION

HELIX

Michael Moorcock's
MULTIVERSE
PREVIEW

Moonbeams and Roses WALTER SIMONSON
Ridinghood Delacroix MARK REEVE
DUKE ELRIC JOHN RIDGWAY

Elric
AT THE END OF TIME

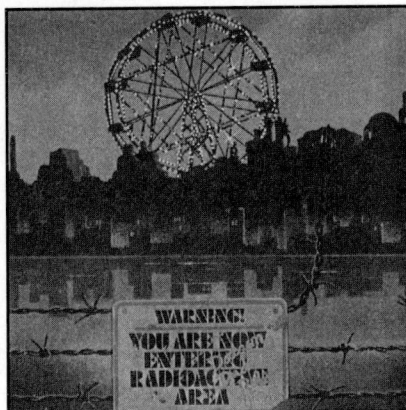

WARNING!
YOU ARE NOW
ENTERED
RADIOACTIVE
AREA

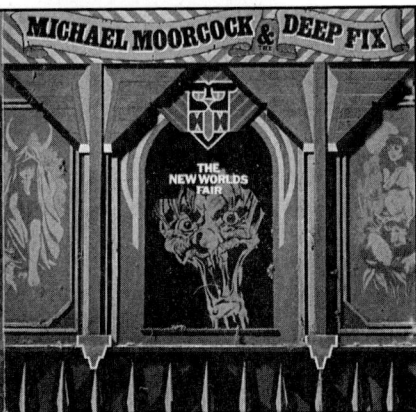

MICHAEL MOORCOCK & DEEP FIX

THE
NEW WORLDS
FAIR

A HEADPRESS BOOK
First published by Headpress in 2014

{t} 0845 330 1844 {e} headoffice@headpress.com

THE LAW OF CHAOS
the Multiverse of Michael Moorcock

Text copyright © Jeff Gardiner
Introduction © Michael Moorcock
This volume copyright © Headpress 2014
Cover painting & design: Janos Orban, courtesy Clonefront Entertainment Ltd.
<arpad@clonefront.co.uk> <http://clonefront.co.uk>
Moorcock portraits: Malcolm Laverty (pp. i, 2, 163) and Bob Covington (p.162)
Book layout: Ganymede Foley
Headpress diaspora: David Kerekes, Thomas Campbell, Caleb Selah,
Giuseppe, Dave T. The publisher wishes to thank Savoy Books.

A CIP catalogue record for this book is available from
the British Library

ISBN 978-1-909394-19-3 (*paperback*)
ISBN 978-1-909394-20-9 (*ebook*)
NO ISBN (*hardback*)

NO ISBN SPECIAL EDITION

Headpress. The gospel according to unpopular culture.
NO ISBN special edition hardbacks and other items are
available exclusively from World Headpress

WWW.WORLDHEADPRESS.COM

BV - #0096 - 110521 - C0 - 203/127/14 - PB - 9781909394193 - Matt Lamination